THE GOOD LIFE
Sacramento's Consumer Culture

Wanted—A Washing Machine

There comes a day in the aver...
American family when Mrs.
...Gray looks up from her cof-
... cup to Mr. Jim Gray, who sits
...cealed behind his newspaper,
...says, "Jim, there is nothing
...it; we have just got to have a
...hing machine." His conscious-
...s penetrated by the despera-
... of that tone. Jim looks around
... paper, whistles a bit, and then
...lies: "Well, my dear, if we've
...to, why I guess we can. What
...of a machine do you want?"
...Mrs. Jim falters a bit, and an-
...ers hesitatingly. "Why—er—any
...that is good."
...Thereupon Mr. Jim Gray sub-
...des into his newspaper.
..."When you have made up your
...let me know, and I guess we
...fix it."
...That is it, what kind? When
...choose a washing machine be
...that you choose one that

Drink Lots of Water

This question of pure water is
not merely talk, but a very important subject to take into con-
sideration. Water should be made
pure for all purposes of cooking
and drinking in the home. Drinking of course more than cooking,
but you will find food tastes better if water is purified first before the food is cooked. Try
making coffee from percolated
water and you will get a better
idea of the advantages of filtered
water. Inquire about the Duplex
Percolator Service. It is $1.00 per
month.

Sperry Cheese Squares

Cook ½ cup Sperry Germea in
2 cups of water 30 min. Turn in
shallow pan. Cover with flaked
Cream O' Gold Cheese. Heat in
oven until melted. Cut in squares
as garnish for Peerless Corned

French Drip Coffee

French drip coffee is perhaps
the best way to serve any coffee. One can procure a pot for
making it that way at Roller's.
But no matter how one makes coffee, one should be very careful
about the quantity used and the
KIND. The quantity is usually
about a tablespoon to a cup. This
varies according to the strength
desired. And as to the kind, there
is no better coffee on the market
to-day than Motor Vacuum Packed
Coffee, and if you will use the
proper quantity, no matter how
you make it, you will get good
results. Ask your grocer for
Motor Coffee next time. Blended,
roasted and packed right in Sacramento.

A Capital Luncheon

The Capital Biscuit Company

Royal Gem Peach Dessert

Sift 2 cups ROYAL GEM FLOUR,
...g teaspoons baking powder,
...teaspoon salt, ½ teaspoon soda;
add ... tablespoons Crystal Butter
and 1 cup sour milk. Arrange
"Our Taste" Peaches in buttered
baking dish seasoned with sugar,
cinnamon, and bits of butter. Cover
top with dough and steam. Serve
hot with cream and sugar.

They Like Them

Little sister or little brother
might turn up their stubby nose
with disdain when plain boiled or
baked potatoes were passed, but
I have never seen the young...
yet, who let the potato chip bowl
pass without trying to take ...
many as his plate would hold.
Keep lots of Crispy Potato Chips
on hand. They are good, and
good for them.

THE GOOD LIFE
Sacramento's Consumer Culture

STEVEN M. AVELLA

ARCADIA
PUBLISHING

Published by Arcadia Publishing,
Charleston SC, Chicago IL, Portsmouth NH, San Francisco CA

Printed in the United States

Library of Congress control number: 2007943616

For all general information contact Arcadia Publishing at:
Telephone 843-853-2070
Fax 843-853-0044
E-Mail sales@arcadiapublishing.com
For customer service and orders:
Toll-Free 1-888-313-2665

Visit us on the Internet at www.arcadiapublishing.com

Unless otherwise noted, images are courtesy of the Sacramento Archives and Museum
Collection Center. Advertisements are from the *Sacramento Bee*, 1910–1985.

To the memory of

DAVID LUBIN, SACRAMENTAN (1849–1919)

who provided for the material needs of his fellow citizens
and tried to feed the hungry of the world

CONTENTS

Acknowledgments

The Good Life began with a request from Jim Kempert of Arcadia Publishing to consider another Sacramento-based title. I floated the idea of doing this book on mass consumption, using Arcadia's popular format to explore an important dimension of Sacramento's culture. Jim agreed and this book took shape.

I incurred a lot of debts in the course of writing this text.

First, I would like to acknowledge the community of scholars and researchers whose ideas and insights on mass consumption in American life I have been able to apply to the Sacramento experience. I tried to mention them in the text whenever I quoted from them or used their ideas. A listing of the main works consulted is at the back of the text.

The images I selected came primarily from the rich collections of the Sacramento Archives and Museum Collection Center (SAMCC) in Sacramento. I wish to acknowledge Marcia Eymann, Patricia Johnson, Carson Hendricks, Dylan McDonald, and Lisa Prince—all of whom gave generously of their time and expertise in helping select and scan these priceless photos. Outgoing director James Henley was often on hand to help me out and I was able to borrow from his work on department stores, which appeared in the *Sacramento History Journal.*

Photos from the collections at the Sacramento Room of the Central Library and the California Room of the State Library were also included. The Sacramento Room, ably directed by Clare Ellis, has always been and continues to be a godsend to scholars of this community.

Thanks to an old friend, John Orr, I was able to make contact with two of Sacramento's legendary home builders, Carroll Brock and James Streng. These phone interviews were a treasure trove of information, as were my informal conversations with John and another friend, Libby Smith, who told me much about Parker Development. To them all, heartfelt gratitude!

Two local historians, *emeritus* professor Gregg Campbell of Sacramento State and Dr. Alfred Yee, graciously read the drafts and offered helpful critique and correction. If any mistakes remain in the text, they are my sole responsibility.

Annette Kassis, a good friend and a historian-in-the-making, plunged into the cold waters of historical research and provided marvelous information on a number of topics. She was especially helpful in using family connections to let me see some of the documents of the business dealings of her famous in-laws. She will be a great historian one day.

Finally, a large portion of the research and the arduous task of moving this book from idea to completion fell into the capable hands of Susan Silva. Susan is competent and patient—perfect qualifications for the demands of this kind of work. I don't know what I would have done without her.

There are many more who deserve thanks—librarians, archivists, and other "midwives" of historical narratives. A generic thanks seems hardly enough—but from my heart, I give it.

Introduction

Charles K. "C. K." McClatchy lived in Sacramento his entire life (1858 to 1936) and was a keen observer of the city's changes over the years. In a 1925 column, the *Sacramento Bee* editor remarked on the quality of life of his fellow Sacramentans: "Life never was fuller of more varied instruments for the use not of the select few, but of the greatest multitude. An American workingman has at his command that [which] a Croesus once could not purchase. In our country at least there is a level of general comfort which never has been attained before."

After World War I, Sacramento, like the rest of the nation, had embraced a "culture of consumption." As never before, Sacramentans could purchase and consume a wide array of affordable, mass produced goods and services to meet their basic needs of food, shelter, clothing, and transportation. In addition, city residents now had the means to buy "luxuries" like radios, automobiles, refrigerators, and a host of other goods. Where they bought these things changed over time, too. From small shops and business enterprises, Sacramento's retail outlets became larger and more elaborate—lavishly and attractively displaying the wide array of goods they wished to sell. Although the Great Depression and World War II slowed the momentum of consumption, it resumed during the postwar period and has never stopped.

Mass consumption was not unique to Sacramento. It was a national and even international phenomenon, which this book examines on a local scale, providing an overview of Sacramento's changing habits of consumerism during the twentieth century. This is a history "from the bottom up," for all Sacramentans were shoppers. This approach also highlights the contributions of merchants and retailers, the middlemen of Sacramento's culture of mass consumption, whose investments, creativity, successes, and failures left an important imprint on the city's life and culture. Many of their names were once emblazoned on their businesses and became a part of Sacramento's common lexicon: Weinstock, Lubin, Breuner, Arata, Corti, Raley, and Swift—just to name a few.

The significance of mass consumption is often reflected in people's anecdotal memories of the city. Oral histories frequently evoke experiences of shopping downtown, along J or K Streets. Early suburbanites reminisce about driving to Town & Country Village or Country Club Centre in the 1950s to buy the latest apparel at these first shopping centers. Some remember shopping for groceries at Sacramento favorites like Stop 'n Shop or Arata Brothers. Others recall the array of Chinese-run markets that once dotted the community. Jingles and merchandising campaigns impressed brand names on the buying public via radio and television broadcasts and print advertisements in the newspapers.

The Good Life is not a comprehensive history of Sacramento consumerism. It only samples by text, historic photos, and reproduced ads, some of the agencies and people associated with mass consumption in the region.

In addition, it also notes the contribution of Sacramento to the dynamic mass production that made American industries the envy of the globe. The city railroad yards manufactured railroad cars and engines that transported goods across the continent. An array of canneries processed fruits and vegetables from nearby fields into canned foods sold around the country and the world. Sacramentans tested rocket engines, made boxes and cans, produced soap products, and milled rice for the international market. Today they design computer hardware and software. With their earnings, Sacramentans still purchase food, clothing, homes, cars, vacations, and entertainment.

The quality of life in Sacramento has often been defined by the kinds of things Sacramentans could buy. What "Croesus once could not purchase" has often been at the fingertips of Sacramentans of the twentieth and twenty-first centuries.

1. "THE SELLING FORCE"
Mass Consumption, Sacramento-Style

Human beings have always consumed—food, shelter, clothing—but mass consumption is a by-product of the revolution that occurred in industrial technology, transportation, communication, and organization during the late nineteenth and early twentieth centuries. Mass production transformed American life, creating huge cities and requiring large workforces, new infrastructures, and governmental reforms. Mass production lowered the per-unit cost of most goods and factory wages made it possible for workers and others to purchase what the industries produced. Advertising, improved marketing, and better transportation brought these goods into the homes of American consumers.

The work of archaeologists Mary and Adrian Praetzellis on a home at 808 I Street in Sacramento reveals the imprint of mass consumption patterns in the state capital. The 1988 excavation of the refuse-filled cellar of the home, torn down in 1905 and owned by one Mary Collins, "shows the influence of mass marketing on the purchasing habits of the Collins household." The artifacts discovered indicate that "the Collins family had a preference for nationally advertised products." These included a "larger number of products from the lower quality grades." The Praetzellises note, "the Collins collection reflects the purchasing pattern of a lower middle class household in the early years of the consumer revolution."

Sacramentans Produce

Sacramento participated in the dynamic, mass production economy that transformed America in the late nineteenth and early twentieth centuries. Railroad repair and construction were among the city's first major industries. The Sacramento railroad yards were located north of the city's central business district along "Sutter's Lake" and eventually encompassed 240

Once one of the largest manufacturing centers in the West, the Sacramento rail yards produced cars, engines, and other mechanical equipment. It also paid wages to thousands of Sacramentans.

acres. This repair and construction site was for a time the largest industrial manufacturing center west of St. Louis. Thousands of local workers labored in its various departments: the lumber mill, blacksmith shop, rolling mill, or other manufacturing facilities. From 1873 to 1937 the shops manufactured locomotives, some of them the primary engines for the romantically-named routes of the Southern Pacific—the *Coast Daylight*, *City of San Francisco*, *Cascade Limited*, and *Golden State*. A number of elegant Pullman rail cars also rolled out of the shops, as well as streetcars, engines, and other transportation equipment. As one historian of the yards has noted, the railroad exercised the "single greatest influence on Sacramento's economy until government became big business in the capital city."

Canning was another major industry—perhaps the one that best exemplifies the mass production techniques of the industrial age. The fruit of Sacramento Valley's fields and orchards flowed into the city, where it was processed and transported to markets all over the nation and abroad. If Sacramentans could purchase textiles from Chicago and kerosene refined in a Standard Oil plant in Cleveland, Missourians and Hoosiers could open cans of Sacramento-processed fruits and vegetables for their daily fare. Sacramento's once-flourishing canning industry began in the 1860s with a small fish cannery along the Sacramento River just north of Old Sacramento, which processed salmon. Steady improvements in canning technology and a concomitant improvement in agricultural productivity made the state capital one of the most important centers for canning fruit and vegetables in the nation. In 1906, when the Pacific Fruit Express built a large refrigeration plant in Roseville, the shipping of perishable fruits and vegetables also took off in the area.

By 1924, six major canning plants existed within the city. The California Packing Corporation was the leader, operating two of these huge plants with their trademark Del Monte products. Libby, McNeill & Libby, Smith Frank, and J. P. Hynes operated plants as well.

Sacramento's once thriving canning industry was a prime example of mass production techniques. The Del Monte brand was famous throughout the nation. (This photograph was taken c. 1935.)

The Economic Impact of Sacramento Jobs

Industrial and service labor jobs created steady income for Sacramentans—dollars that they could spend on the basics and even more. By 1919, for example, the railroad employed close to 3,500 workers at its shops, pouring nearly $400,000 into the city from its monthly payroll. In 1919 alone, the railroad injected $3.7 million into Sacramento's economy. By 1952, the Southern Pacific yards still employed 3,100 men and women (women had been recruited for the heavy industrial labor needed during both world wars), pumping $875,000 each month into the region through its payroll. Canneries employed anywhere from 3,000 to 5,000 seasonal workers, many of them women. In 1924 they reported an annual payroll of $1.2 million; by 1930, wages has risen to nearly $3 million.

Military, federal, state, and local government work also contributed to income streams. Three major military installations, Mather Field, McClellan Field, and the Army Signal Depot located permanently in Sacramento in the 1930s, providing thousands of jobs. Beginning in the 1930s and continuing

Sacramento's military bases were a prime source of employment from the 1930s through the 1990s.

to the present day, the expansion of the state government bureaucracy has poured money into the local economy. In 1941, 10,130 Sacramento area residents were employed by various levels of the government, injecting more than $18 million into the local economy. In 2007, government is still the single largest employer of people in the Sacramento area with 221,000 collecting a paycheck from one of its agencies.

During the Great Depression and World War II the pace of employment slowed, with wages stagnating or receding. However, after the war the local economy took off once again, thanks in large measure to the infusion of federal dollars. The per capita income among Sacramentans grew considerably. In 1954, city dwellers earned an average of $2,170, and county residents $1,859 each year. By 1959 city dwellers took in $2,524, and county residents $2,177 annually. Money pumped in by the military bases contributed largely to this surge. The federal government poured in hundreds of millions of dollars to expand and upgrade the bases over the years. By 1955, McClellan Air Force Base had the largest payroll in Sacramento County, $72 million a year. Two years earlier the *Sacramento Bee* noted that base employees made local purchases of around $14 million and had accelerated the development of nearly 2,000 acres near McClellan.

Private firms related to the defense industry also played a significant role. In the 1950s, the aerospace giant Aerojet, which made rocket engines for the federal government, secured a 7,200-acre tract of dredged-out land 16 miles east of the city on the south side of Highway 50, paying a whopping $6.6 million for the new plant. Aerojet's workforce peaked in 1963, giving paychecks to 19,792 employees and accounting for more than 60 percent of the region's manufacturing employment. Decades later, the high-tech revolution of the 1980s and 1990s created thousands of new jobs, paying an average wage of $40,000 per year. In 2007, the two computer giants in the region—Intel Corporation and Hewlett Packard Company—employed around 11,000 people.

Various factors contributed to periods of expansion and decline in the local economy. For example, the closure of the three military installations in the 1990s was a significant blow. However, per capita income grew steadily in Sacramento in the 1980s and 1990s—from a little more than $15,000 in 1986 to nearly $25,000 by 1997. It declined a bit by 1999, but by 2005 it was back up to nearly $25,000. These rises in income often meant an increase in buying power for the average Sacramentan.

Retail sales, which stood at $340,876,000 in 1950, more than doubled by 1959 to $735,175,000. By 2005, retail sales in Sacramento County had exceeded $21.25 billion a year.

Borrowing and Credit

The extension of credit also contributed to the expansion of mass consumption. At any time, few Sacramentans had the financial resources to pay cash for big-ticket items like houses and automobiles. Eventually, however, credit possibilities loosened up as the purveyors of cars, major appliances, and even luxuries like jewelry extended credit to worthy customers. "Buying on time," or installment buying, became as much a part of Sacramento's consumer ethos as it was all over the nation.

Easy credit terms allowed families to purchase high-priced items like automobiles.

Installment buying had been around for a while. Farm equipment was purchased this way in the nineteenth century, as were Singer sewing machines. The General Motors Acceptance Corporation, founded in 1919, provided one of the first credit bureaus for would-be car buyers. GM auto dealers like Sterling P. Forrest, the owner of one of Sacramento's largest Chevrolet franchises, wrote in a full page ad in the 1920s, "I would estimate that 75 percent of all cars purchased, are bought on the installment plan. . . . If you decide on a Chevrolet, I can handle the transaction on terms that will be *easy and convenient*, and you should have no hesitancy in letting me know if you prefer credit."

In the post–World War II era credit purchases increased, and between 1946 and 1958, short term consumer credit quintupled. One of the factors contributing to this was the widespread use of the credit card, which provided an easy way of making purchases. The Diners Club card first appeared in 1951. In 1958, American Express issued a card, and in 1959 the first Bank of America cards (later VISA) were advertised to the public. In 1967, the Western States Bankcard Association formed and introduced MasterCharge (later MasterCard). Sears issued the Discover card in 1985. It is difficult to establish when and where Sacramentans first used credit cards, but major retailers soon accepted them and even began issuing their own charge plates. Steady improvements in the recording of credit card purchases, i.e., electronic readers and magnetic strips, eventually extended the facility of credit card purchases to virtually every product, including groceries and gasoline as well as purchases on the Internet. Incentives to adopt these credit cards now flood the mailbox of the typical consumer, sweetened with added enticements such as air miles or points for future discounts. The plastic filling the typical consumer's wallet represents thousands of dollars of credit.

Home buying, the largest single purchase many Americans ever make, has been substantially boosted by federal and state loan guarantees. The policies of the Veteran's Administration and the Federal Housing Administration released a torrent of capital allowing people to purchase homes. The federal tax deduction for mortgage interest provided another incentive to home buying. In addition, liberalized home equity loans contributed to the availability of ready cash for many middle-class people, increasing their capacity to spend. Automobile and personal loans by banks and savings and loan associations have underwritten the purchase of durables and financed everything from college educations to vacations. Sacramentans, like other Americans, often lived on a pile of debt, but they enjoyed the many comforts and conveniences of the good life.

The Role of Advertising

Mass consumption is also linked to the rise of modern advertising and the dissemination of its messages in print, radio, television, and now cyberspace. Historian Roland Marchand in *Advertising the American Dream* (1985) asserted that modern advertising created needs that many never knew they had—for household appliances, hygienic products, fashionable clothing, automobiles, and many other products. Advertising became more sophisticated as research on motivation added to the skills of marketers. Using this research, subtle and skillful advertisers created a collective momentum behind certain products that were "indispensable" for good living and the maintenance of social status.

Sacramento was subject to the various waves of advertising that marketed products nationally and even internationally. The primary medium of early advertising in Sacramento during the first decades of the twentieth century was newsprint, specifically the two daily newspapers, the *Sacramento Bee* and the *Sacramento Union*. Both papers had active advertising departments and competed with one another to sell space on their pages. The clear leader in advertising was the evening *Sacramento Bee,* thanks in large measure to the skillful efforts of Valentine S. "V. S." McClatchy, the paper's co-publisher and business manager until his departure in 1923. Newspaper advertising took on increasing sophistication over the course of time as ads moved from the front pages to the interiors of the paper, often occupying full pages, and later separate sections and inserts, sometimes in full color. Commercial artists drew wonderful pictures of products and storefronts for daily editions. New store openings, seasonal sales, and price reductions or service expansions were also well displayed. Eventually a substantial Sunday edition, filled with discount coupons and colorful inserts, increased the reach of the *Bee* and encouraged

Handsomely drawn ads like this 1910 advertisement for Colonial Heights no doubt helped spur home sales.

further mass consumption. Some advertisers used billboards, found all over the area, and even today Sacramentans can see the traces of elaborate advertisements once painted on the exterior walls of city buildings.

Radio and Television

On February 2, 1922, a low wattage radio service, KVQ, began Sacramento's radio era with a brief broadcast. This early station went off the air after a short time, unable to make itself heard to a wide enough audience. Kimball-Upson, a local sporting-goods store, and the *Sacramento Union* picked up the facility as a joint venture and created a 500-watt station, by then known as KFBK. Eventually the McClatchy Company, owner of the *Sacramento Bee* and other media, purchased the station and extended the range of its advertising beyond the city.

Radio and television advertising took mass consumption to new heights. Distinctive music, jingles, and images were used to create consumer demand.

Telegrams pouring in from Yreka, Susanville, and even Reno demonstrated the reach of the station. The initial broadcasts were limited to Monday, Thursday, and Saturday nights from 7:30 until 9:00, but as time went on the broadcasts expanded to the entire week and for longer periods during the day. This new medium provided another forum for advertising the goods and services of local merchants. It also boosted the sales of radios themselves— one of the major consumer items of the 1920s and 1930s. The broadcast of popular sporting events in retail radio stores such as Breuner's, the Sherman-Clay Company, and the Tussinger Radio Store, introduced people to these products. People could also hear broadcasts at service stations, used car lots, and a downtown cyclery.

Local merchants like the auto dealership Arnold Brothers sponsored a musical group called the Hudson-Essex String Trio, which played "old-time" favorites like *Sweet Rosie O'Grady*, *The Sidewalks of New York*, and *Where the*

River Shannon Flows as a contrast to modern jazz and "heavy" classical music. The brothers hoped that the "old-fashioned listeners" would be interested in their automobiles. Hart's Cafeteria at 919 K Street, a popular downtown eatery, also sponsored a live orchestra that broadcast semi-classical music and invitations to dine at their establishment.

In 1937, local Dodge dealer Royal Miller began radio station KROY (named for himself), broadcasting from studios on the mezzanine of the Hotel Sacramento at Tenth and K. By 1945, stations KCRA and KXOA had joined KFBK and KROY. Each of them was affiliated with national radio networks NBC (KCRA), Mutual (KXOA), ABC (KFBK), and CBS (KROY), all of which opened Sacramento even wider to national advertising programs. Advertising jingles, rhymes, and plugs for certain products by popular entertainers further increased consumption.

The advent of television in the 1950s created a tremendous transformation in mass consumption in Sacramento. In the 1980s, the advance of cable television with its plethora of stations, some of which, like the shopping network, were devoted entirely to advertising, had a powerful effect on Sacramento consumers. Sophisticated filmed advertisements of various products—cars, makeup, furniture, and food—stimulated consumption as never before. A great deal of this came through national ad campaigns.

Branding

The creation of an identity by associating names, symbols, logos, and jingles with products was useful to companies seeking to press the distinctiveness of their products in highly competitive markets. Products having brand recognition created consumer loyalty. In some cases, brand names actually became synonymous with the product itself—familiar names like Crisco, Kleenex, and Vaseline are examples.

Sacramento businesses had their share of brand recognition. Crystal creamery, whose first churning operation was located at 728 K Street, was a familiar name among Sacramentans for generations. Carl F. Hansen purchased Crystal in 1921 from George Gordon Knox and Associates of San Francisco, who had incorporated the business in 1901. The Crystal Cream

These are two popular Sacramento brands. Blue Diamond Almonds, above, are still processed in the city. The beer ad below provides a visual of the product's ascent after the end of Prohibition.

& Butter Co. remained in the Hansen family until May 2007 when they sold it to one of the largest dairy companies in the United States, HP Hood LLC of Chelsea, Massachusetts. Crystal products carried a distinctively scripted "C" logo, and Sacramentans recognized and associated the logo with Crystal's quality dairy products. Sacramento's two major breweries of the early twentieth century, Ruhstaller and Buffalo, produced local beers that were popular in Sacramento and its environs. Ruhstaller's "Gilt Edge" logo was familiar to Sacramentans. Blue Diamond Almonds have become a national and international favorite. Produced by Blue Diamond Growers, a co-op that began in 1910, these almonds sold well in more than 90 countries in 2007 with gross sales of nearly $2 billion. The city's name graces the label of Sacramento Tomato Juice, a nationally marketed product, produced by Bercut-Richards Packing Company and eventually bought out by Borden in 1968.

Local Sacramento businesses had brand recognition as well. Furniture shopping was for years associated with the name Breuner. Shopping for clothes, shoes, or an umbrella? Weinstock, Lubin & Co. and Hale's carried these products. Pizza was for many years synonymous with the name Shakey and orange freeze with Merlino. Internationally renowned Tower Books and Records meant you had access to the best music and reading materials in your community. The Leatherby name immediately brings to mind ice cream.

Planned and Unplanned Obsolescence

"Planned obsolescence" is the name traditionally attributed to the "model year" strategy of General Motors. This marketing innovation insisted that certain products and styles had to be updated every few years so that consumers would want to remain "up-to-date" and "modern." The newest was always the most improved, and the retention of old-fashioned products was considered a social detriment. Other products imitated this process and affixed "New" and "Improved" on brand labels and in advertising. New styles in fashion became a mainstay of the clothing industry. Fashion shows and concerted marketing campaigns in the spring and fall by clothing

The distinctive logo and the Dutch Maid of Crystal were to be found on many Sacramento tables.

retailers in Sacramento sought to keep women and men up on the latest styles. Twenty-first century consumers probably best understand planned obsolescence through the continual upgrades and replacements of software required to run their personal computers.

Obsolescence has not only been dictated by a continual quest to remain current, nor has it always been due to shifting patterns in public tastes. "Scientific" discoveries have also contributed to a product's demise. In 1921 for example, locals declared the corset "passé" for health and style reasons and invoked "scientific authority" to validate this claim. Lavinia Kaull, supervisor of physical education for the Sacramento City schools, urged women to rid themselves of the confining undergarment for the sake of better health and proper muscle and inner organ development, as well as better respiration: "The fleshy woman who has become a slave to the corset has no idea of the joy that comes with the mastery of all bodily movements." "Followers of style" and buyers in local department stores echoed Kaull's recommendations.

The decline of the canning industry was attributed to the development of frozen foods but even more to the increasing demand for fresh fruits and vegetables, as well as the availability of imported fresh produce. Health conscious consumers wanted fruits and vegetables without the heavy sugar syrups and with the vitamins and nutrients that were to some degree lost in processing. Trucking firms were able to bring in regular supplies of produce to Sacramento grocers, and weekly farmers' markets popped up at various locations throughout the Sacramento area, including the ample parking lots of the region's shopping malls.

Seasons of Consumption

A spot check of any retail mall on a Saturday or Sunday suggests that mass consumption is a year-round phenomenon. However, historian Leigh Eric Schmidt notes the extent to which consumption has "colonized" other aspects of life such as religious and public festivals—celebrations that have no overt link to consumption.

As early as 1920, local businessmen freely offered advice to churchmen who lamented their dwindling congregations. J. B. Coghill, president of the Sacramento Ad Club, in a scene reminiscent of Sinclair Lewis's 1923 classic *Babbitt*, lectured the members of the First Baptist Church, "that there must be something wrong with the selling force of a church that fails to attract the outsider." He urged them to "advertise the gospel of Jesus Christ everywhere." Exhorting the congregation to use newspapers, billboards, and movies, he further stated: "If you'll knock out part of one of those walls and install a moving picture machine, you'll soon find your church filled to overflowing." Coghill's ad-man pitch may have affected the strategies of the congregation, but more often than not, it was the advertisers who used religious holidays as a springboard for their own promotional campaigns.

Consumption patterns tend to spike at different times of the year, often related to religious holidays. The volume of Christmas shopping has become an important economic barometer. Good receipts, especially on the first

K Street, an important retail district, is decked out for the Christmas holidays.

day of the shopping rush after Thanksgiving, augur economic health for retailers. Bad returns suggest the opposite. In Sacramento's history, seasonal celebrations like Christmas, Easter, and Valentine's Day (and even the unique period of civic energy during the annual California State Fair) are days when retailers push hard for sales. Christmas, the Christian feast that celebrates the birth of Jesus Christ, is an intense season of mass consumption. The tradition of gift-giving on the holiday, cultivated in America on December 25 when St. Nicholas/Father Christmas/Santa Claus is supposed to deliver toys and treats to good little children, has created the expectation that everyone should find a present under the tree. Merchants rely heavily on the "Christmas rush" to increase their sales, hoping to end their year comfortably in the black. Sacramento, like other cities, helped to commercialize Christmas. In the 1920s and perhaps even earlier, the local Retailer's Association urged area retailers to accentuate holiday motifs in store windows. Lavish displays in the windows of Weinstock, Lubin & Co. and Breuner's helped to create a festive mood in the downtown shopping district. Memories of those days are often echoed in Sacramentans' recollections of their city. City historian James Henley wrote of the windows, "At one point Breuner's [a local furniture and appliance store on K Street] became the attraction in Sacramento. It almost wasn't Christmas if you didn't go down and see the Breuner's window."

Sacramento had long participated in the commercialization of Christmas, despite repeated complaints of clergy and others that such over-emphasis on buying caused the "reason for the season" to be lost. In a less intense way, shopping frenzies also were encouraged around Easter time, particularly clothiers urging new apparel for Easter Sunday celebrations. Other celebrations like St. Valentine's Day (February 14), Mother's Day (the second Sunday in May), and the Fourth of July inspired other opportunities

a

Valentine

Surprise

by ELIZABETH ARDEN

● This Valentine holds a glad surprise in its satin heart—it contains a crystal and fragrant bottle of Elizabeth Arden Blue Grass perfume. Anything from Elizabeth Arden is sure of a radiant welcome, but even Miss Arden has never sponsored anything so instantly beloved as her Paris-created perfumes. And in this gala Valentine dress there could be no more winning way to say "I love you", $5 or if your heart is larger, $12.50.

Elizabeth Arden

Weinstock-Lubin & Co.

This 1936 Valentine's Day promotion urged suitors to spend at least $5 to say "I love you"— a not inconsiderable sum during the Great Depression.

This interesting Hale's ad attempts to capitalize on the recent election of Republican Warren G. Harding in 1920.

for sales and merchandising. Today, Halloween comes close to Christmas in terms of the amount of retail activity it generates.

The commercialization of Christmas and Easter has raised ambiguous feelings in many who lament that the religious meaning of these holidays is being emptied out in an orgy of shopping.

The Social Impact of Consumption

Sociologist Thorstein Veblen was one of the first to probe the meaning of mass consumption. In his 1899 *The Theory of the Leisure Class*, he argued that consumption was a symbol of status for the elite. Veblen defined "conspicuous consumption" as the acquisition of more and more goods, which bestowed a certain social status on the possessor. What one consumes is often a symbol of one's economic state. Fancy homes, cars, and clothing mark a person of distinction. Ads in Sacramento newspapers for various types of goods appealed to class distinctions or suggested that one who purchased a certain type of merchandise gave evidence of being "high-class."

Consumption was also a window into gender roles. In Sacramento, local commentators suggested that shopping was largely the preserve of the female. For example, a reporter, surveying the men's sections of Sacramento department stores, concluded in a September 1921 article in the *Bee* that women made most of the purchases:

> A man just naturally has not the time to go shopping, or if he does he rushes into a store and demands what he wants, makes certain it is the right size, and without further parley pays for it and rushes out. . . . The wife on the other hand has the time and inclination to go search for the best that can be had for the money. She it is who looks into his dresser drawers and notices that he needs a new shirt or [that] his stiff collars are becoming frayed. . . . God bless the women, if it wasn't for them most husbands would be looking like a rag picker.

Male frustration with the time it took women to shop also suggested genderized shopping roles. "My domestic life runs smoothly," lamented one man dragged to a downtown department store, "until I go shopping with my wife. Then I wonder why I ever got married. Can she make up her mind about a purchase? She can not. She is like the cow—always looking for greener pasture. Now me, I know what I want and I buy it." Although these passages seem ludicrous to the gender-sensitized ears of twenty-first century readers, they reflect how gender roles often define consumption practices and vice versa. Women may have occasionally visited the Kimball-Upson sporting goods store or shopped for lighting and electrical fixtures at Hobrecht's Lighting on Tenth and J Streets, but men probably rarely visited the women's fashion stores Nonpareil at Sixth and K or Reich and Lièvre at Seventh and K.

Women's needs and influence were central to advertising and marketing efforts. Historian Susan Strasser notes that many mass produced consumer

Reich and Lièvre and Weinstock appeal to women shoppers with smartly drawn images of attractive women in elegant apparel. Men too must have perused these ads.

items were designed to create more leisure time for women. For example, mass produced clothing delivered women from the toil and tedium of spinning and sewing. The kitchen was, according to other historians, one of the most popular objects of mass consumption: stoves, refrigerators, and dishwashers all added new levels of convenience and time-saving to a typical middle-class home. One scholar has commented that the inclusion of Home Economics classes in high schools with lessons on clothing, hygiene, and cooking prepared women to be the directors of family consumption.

Youth Markets

Marketers also targeted the growing youth cohort in the nation and in Sacramento. The number of Sacramento's young grew dramatically after World War II, affecting not only the city's educational and health-care institutions but also retailers, who recognized that the growing market for clothing, shoes, food, sports equipment, toys, movies, and other youth paraphernalia meant big profits. Television and radio facilitated their efforts. Both newspaper and television ads—especially the advertising on local afternoon kiddie shows like Captain Sacto, Skipper Stu, and other programs of the 1950s—created a reservoir of demand that helped television become a leading medium in the United States. By 1955 spending for television advertisements hit $1 billion nationally. Sacramento's three major television stations—KCRA, KXTV, and KOVR—all relied extensively on advertising income to underwrite their broadcasts. National marketing came via the major networks and local firms bought air time to advertise their products.

Sacramento parents shopped for school clothes and children's toys—bikes, baseballs, dolls, etc.—in the children's sections of local department stores. Toys were also purchased at Toyland at 818 J Street or later at Kid-E Korrall in Town & Country Village and the Country Club Centre. Youth-oriented restaurant chains began catering to young people. Shakey's Pizza, which originated in Sacramento in 1954, was quite popular with teenagers from the 1960s onward.

Sacramento actually became an important center for youth-targeted marketing with the advent of Russ Solomon's Tower Records, which began

Advertisers targeted the growing youth population of America especially after World War II. Their purchases of clothing, records, and cosmetics were a major part of the booming U.S. economy.

in a drugstore located in the Tower Theater building in the 1940s. Its first stand-alone store opened in 1960 on Watt Avenue. Tower catered to a variety of musical tastes, but was especially popular with youth who could purchase popular singles and longer-playing records of their favorite musicians. Top Forty music blared continuously from the popular KXOA-AM radio, which began broadcasting top rock-and-roll tunes in the 1950s, and later KROY, which switched to the same format in 1960. The proliferation of youth-oriented AM and FM radio has no doubt contributed to the enormous sums spent each year from the 1970s onward by Sacramento youth on everything from beauty aids and music to concerts and clothing. Eventually, shopping malls became the favorite hangouts for school-age youth, replacing soda fountains and movie theaters.

By the 1990s, savvy youths would also be among those who led the way in the use of the Internet, a major source of shopping outlets, as well as the purchasing of digital entertainment and video games. Certain industries, such as books, electronics, clothing, and jewelry have experienced important spikes in sales thanks to the convenience of Internet shopping.

Consumption Reorders Urban Space

City space was arranged to facilitate the priority of mass consumption. Sacramento's retail districts have evolved over the course of time. From the non-differentiated districts along the embarcadero, the city developed an early merchant's row running east along J and K Streets. The city's inexorable eastward growth eventually drew the business district with it. The improvement of city streets and transport systems and the increasing rationalization of the city into zones in the 1920s created a retail district farther east on J and K Streets. All of the businesses that had been located west of Fifth Street began to look for new properties in the prime area.

Department stores hosted visits with popular Disney characters as a way of bringing young customers and their parents into the stores.

Harry Thorp, the president of Weinstock, Lubin & Co. from 1906 to 1916, wrote about this in his 1912 annual report:

> Perhaps the most detrimental local factor affecting business at the present time and for months past, is the general up-town movement. The erection of magnificent buildings in the neighborhood of Eighth Street, like the Forum, Nicolaus, Hales, and People's Bank Building, as well as being the terminal of two important electric lines, all of which had the tendency to swing trade away from 4th and K and establish the foregoing locality as "the shopping center." As a natural result competition has increased in this district and throughout the city. Looking backwards, we seem to have completely overlooked this up-town development, otherwise an effort would have been made to counteract this move by some outward signs of life in the direction of improving our adjacent sixty feet of K Street property, or equipping our plants with conspicuous electric advertising signs, or some other device likely to bring the crowd down this way, and act as a continuous advertising magnet after dark. We must do something additional to keep this end of town attractive and interesting. Up to the present we have looked on with complacency, and wondered at the strides made by our neighbors.

Sacramento's growing use of the automobile also created new zones of consumption. The downtown shopping district worked hard to accommodate shoppers who came in cars. "The automobile has become the big factor in bringing the modern stores and throbbing shopping districts within a few hours radius of the man and his family fifty miles or more away," wrote the *Bee* in 1921. Later, the automobile drew people out of the city center to its peripheries where new retail districts helped to define the metropolitan landscape.

The post–World War II suburban expansion of Sacramento to the northeast and south meant the relocation of various shopping districts. These districts

The Weinstock Lubin Store at Twelfth and K was one of the most elegant of Sacramento's downtown department stores.

included automobile sales and service; grocery and department stores followed their markets. Shopping centers such as the 1946 Town & Country Village at Fulton and Marconi, and the 1952 Country Club Centre at El Camino and Watt led the way in the creation of suburban shopping districts. Former state historian and part-time Sacramento resident Kevin Starr noted the ongoing diffusion of shopping districts and their effects on Sacramento's development. In the final volume of his 2004 California history series, *Coast of Dreams*, he wrote of Sacramento's metropolitan evolution: "From the air, or even from Highways 99 and 5 or Interstates 5 and 880, the region looked like a city in its continuous weaving of shopping-center oriented suburban communities." With his legendary gift of rhetorical breadth, Starr observed, "in terms of its social-spatial arrangements, metro Sacramento was most fundamentally a mall- and shopping center-oriented kind of a place, with the Arden Mall at the intersection of Interstate 80 and Arden Way serving as the *de facto* civic center of the region."

Mass consumption defined the culture of twentieth and twenty-first century American life. Sacramento was part of the wider national experience, and its identity and existence were wrapped up in this experience. Sacramentans shopped for cars, food, shelter, and clothing within this context.

2. "You Can't Live Without Them Here"
Automobiles

Sacramentans love cars. By 1940 automobile registrations in the county exceeded 60,000, and the retailing of new and used automobiles was the largest single business in the city as 17 firms marketed to the area. At the end of 2006 there were more than 2.7 million vehicles in the Sacramento area and each home had an average of two vehicles. Auto sales have generally been very strong in Sacramento County. In 2006, nearly 10 percent of Sacramentans anticipated buying a new vehicle.

Automobiles are one of the most important emblems of mass production and consumption in American life. After a home, they are the second largest expenditure most consumers make. The mass production and sale of automobiles has been attributed to the inventive and organizational genius of Henry Ford, whose assembly-line techniques placed the horseless carriage within reach of middle-class Americans. The Model T cost $950 in 1909. By 1924, the price had dropped to $290. Later, installment buying and other forms of credit caused sales to spike even more. The insurance, fuel, and ongoing maintenance of automobiles are in themselves major industries.

The widespread use of the automobile has changed the way Americans live in very visible ways. It has reworked public spaces by requiring the building of newer and wider roads and more and bigger parking lots. It has enabled the growth of the suburbs and the exurbs. It has created new venues for shopping, entertainment, and even church going. It has also meant the decreasing use of public transportation. Sacramento adapted very easily to the advent of automobiles, and Sacramento consumers bought autos at very rapid rates—sometimes more extensively than any other part of California.

The Automobile Comes to the Capital: Car Sales and Culture Before 1945

The west coast was slow to take to the automobile. Historian Joseph McGowan noted that even though there were automobiles in other parts of the United States in 1896, "none were to be found on the west coast." The automobile made its initial appearance as a curiosity piece, perhaps first seen in Sacramento in 1898 and 1899 when a circus brought an electric automobile as an attraction. In May 1900, a street fair also displayed an automobile as a technological curiosity. A few months later, during the California State Fair, Sacramento had its first automobile race, sponsored by San Francisco merchants. This competition had cars circling the mile track at the Agricultural Park in two minutes and twenty-nine seconds—a bit slower than the race horses.

Public celebrations soon integrated automobiles into parades and demonstrations. In May 1902, three cars were entered into the city's

Sacramento had its own auto manufacturing operation for a brief time. The Golden West Motors Factory on Seventh Avenue and Riverside turned out heavy-duty trucks. The company disappeared around 1920. (Courtesy Sacramento Room, Sacramento Public Library.)

The Ford

"The Car of Satisfaction"

Has ten horse power -- weighs one thousand pounds.

Reliable, efficient, powerful, easily controlled. Simple construction, parts easy of access, handsome, large roomy seats, no noise, no vibration, smooth running, comfortable, minimum fuel consumption, minimum cost of maintenance, maximum efficiency. $600 less than any other automobile with a double opposed motor.

Veach Novelty Works, Agents, Sacramento, Cal.

This view of an early Sacramento auto was taken in front of the capitol. In its early appearance, the automobile was appropriately marketed by a novelty company. (Courtesy California History Room, California State Library, Sacramento.)

annual Floral Parade. During the State Fair of 1905, a Grand Auto Parade Extravaganza was held on September 6, featuring more than 100 automobiles. According to the September 7, 1905 edition of the *Sacramento Union*, "the grand showing certainly did more to bring the automobile in favor than a dozen years of indiscriminately running over innocent people and frightening crazy horses." In 1916, to celebrate the dedication of the new Immaculate Conception Church in Oak Park, William F. Gormley led a score of vehicles from the downtown to the new church. Bishop Thomas Grace arrived in a rented taxi.

According to city directories, the first automobile agency in Sacramento began in 1903 with a company headed by Joseph J. Schnerr, who sold automobiles and bicycles. Schnerr later teamed up with Lew E. Nickell to expand sales. They also opened one of the first auto repair shops in Sacramento. In 1905 California began registering automobiles. Of the 2,475 cars in the state, Sacramento had 27. From 1905 forward, sales of automobiles and accommodations for them in the city took off. Already by 1906, the Arnold Brothers had opened a car dealership in the city, eventually

The small print in this wonderfully drawn Chevrolet brand advertisement promises a small down payment and convenient terms.

becoming the main supplier of Hudson and Essex automobiles all over northern California. By 1910, there were more than 700 cars in Sacramento County. By July 1911, Sacramentans were buying new automobiles at a rate of 75 a month. In 1914 there were 9,184 automobiles registered in the Sacramento Valley and the foothills. That number soared to 17,907 in 1916, 25,000 by 1917, 32,000 in 1918, 42,000 in 1919, and nearly 50,000 by 1920.

In 1919, after a brief downturn in business because of the war, auto dealers reported that they were unable to keep up with demand. In 1923, Sacramento's automobile business gained a whopping 560 percent for February when contrasted with the previous year's sales (this amounted to 270 vehicles). In 1925, more than 5,700 cars were purchased in Sacramento County. In October 1926, Sacramento led the nation in the number of automobiles per inhabitant, with one car for every 2.8 citizens—edging out even the large eastern cities.

Sacramentans continually sought newer and more modern cars. New models were touted at the annual auto shows, and Sacramentans (along with the rest of America) awaited the day when the latest "mechanical marvels" would be wheeled into the showrooms of the growing number of dealerships in the city. In 1908, Sacramento staged its first auto show in the State Fair pavilion. W. J. Mannix displayed a new Maxwell and H. D. Arnold a White Steamer. By May 1912, the annual auto show sported 20 different kinds of vehicles. The three-day event began with a parade of cars through downtown to the fairgrounds. Beginning in 1930, a show was held every February in the Memorial Auditorium. Given the mixed urban and rural nature of the county, the displays included trucks, which were still useful to the area's farmers and ranchers. The annual auto show held at the State Fair drew thousands of admiring Sacramentans. The air of excitement around the new models was evident in the roll-out of the 1941 models. A breathless article entitled "New Model Fever" in an August 1940 edition of the *Sacramento Bee* reported: "The entire automotive fraternity is buzzing with reports, rumors and predictions of what this make or that will feature for 1941, and the public is doing as much eavesdropping as it can on this talk."

The consumers of 1925 favored Ford cars (1,119), while Chevrolet (780), Star (636), and Dodge (579) followed. A sample survey taken in August 1926 revealed that of the 488 cars purchased that month in Sacramento County, 120 were Fords. Many were purchased at Moeller Auto Sales, whose dealership at Twelfth and K was popular with Sacramentans. From 1916 until he sold out in 1926, Sterling Forrest's Chevrolet shop, also at Twelfth and K, was a leading General Motors dealership in the city.

Cars were displayed in showrooms or outdoor lots. Car salesmen escorted interested customers to a potential model, and after some form of inspection that usually included a brief test drive, helped to negotiate a deal. The major car companies imposed guidelines and regulations—and quotas—on dealers who marketed their products. The basics of auto retailing did not change much over the years even though the physical size and number of dealerships grew.

The Impact of Automobile Ownership on Sacramento

The increasing rates of automobile ownership and use transformed life in the Sacramento region. In 1925, *Sacramento Bee* editor C. K. McClatchy noted the circumstances at a Fourth of July fireworks celebration at Southside Park. He observed that "the streets for blocks and blocks . . . were packed with parked automobiles frequently parked two abreast on each side of the street." Although he himself was a proud automobile owner (and a speed-demon on the county roads), McClatchy recalled almost wistfully: "Not so many years ago, 'the assembled multitude' would have gone to that scene in family buggies or on foot. . . . No longer is the automobile a luxury. It has developed into an absolute necessity."

Public garages dotted the urban grid. In 1920, the *Bee* reported a building spree of close to $1 million for garages in the state capital. Store owners in the upper K Street retail district were especially anxious to have nearby parking accommodations for customers. According to the paper: "The full length of L Street below Tenth is used more or less for garages and accessory stores, they have spread to M Street as far out as Twenty-ninth; J Street above Tenth has dozens of garages." Permits for private garages for existing homes and the addition of garage plans for newly-constructed dwellings also grew during the 1920s.

Auto traffic competed with Sacramento's public transportation lines. Although streetcars and inter-urban electric trains held their own for a while, they began their slow, steady decline. As early as 1913, trucks replaced horse-drawn teams and even river barges in the hauling of freight. Daily newspapers like the *Bee* and the *Union* developed a fleet of gasoline powered trucks to take their newspapers to areas around the city with greater rapidity than ever before.

City leaders worked steadily to assure the safe and efficient flow of automobile traffic. Policemen appeared at busy intersections to direct motorists, and eventually automated traffic signals were installed. To prevent collisions with other cars and pedestrians, officers issued speeding citations. Railroad crossings sometimes lacked (or motorists ignored) warning bells and safety gates, causing ghastly accidents. Parking on city streets posed problems. In 1945, the first parking meters appeared.

This 1922 photograph illustrates the growing use of police officers for traffic control. (Courtesy California History Room, California State Library, Sacramento.)

Good Roads

The growing popularity and accessibility of automobiles accelerated the pressure for better roads not only in the city but also in the hinterlands. Local bicycle clubs, like the Sacramento Wheelmen and others, had already created a "Good Roads" movement that lobbied for the reconstruction of Sacramento's road system. State government responded with the creation of a Bureau of Highways in March 1895 (renamed the Department of Highways in 1897), which investigated the financing and maintenance of roads in various counties. In 1907, Sacramento passed an $825,000 bond issue that approved a countywide program of road and bridge reconstructions. Improved roads and bridges replaced old thoroughfares east to Folsom, south to Stockton, and to Plymouth. In 1912 funds were set aside for the construction of a bridge over the American River, connecting Fair Oaks to the Folsom Road.

Progressive Governor Hiram Johnson (1910–1917) took on the transportation monopoly created by the railroad companies. Removing Southern Pacific's political and economic control allowed the state to construct public roads and move forward. In 1909 the California Highway Commission was established with authority to create and maintain a state highway system. An $18 million bond passed by a vote of 90,297 to 80,509, with Sacramento County approving it by a vote of 5,284 to 385. A bond issue in 1910 resulted in the building of the Yolo Causeway in 1916, giving Sacramento better access to Yolo and Solano Counties and providing a direct auto route to the East Bay and the ferry to San Francisco. In the summer of 1916, Governor Johnson devoted a week in August to press for good roads. The highlight of the week was a huge automobile parade in the city, covering 37 blocks with 500 vehicles. It drew representatives from Elk Grove, Florin, Galt, Del Paso, Folsom, and Dixon. By 1930, the automobile would knit these heretofore remote areas into a formal metropolitan area.

Automobile Tourism

The automobile made it easier to "market" Sacramento as a tourist hub. In the 1920s, the *Sacramento Bee* added a popular automotive section to its paper that included articles on suggested road trips to nearby locations for Sunday drives or family vacations. One trip, planned for "some cool Autumn evening" included a guided tour of the eastern portion of the county. The article directed the motorist to travel along Twelfth Street to the north, crossing over the American River bridge past North Sacramento, and to zoom past Ben Ali and the Del Paso Municipal Park. A stop at the park for a round of golf or a picnic might be in order, or the auto tourist might drive past the Twelve Mile House to Greenback Road, through the Sacramento County "citrus belt" in Orangevale, and across the newly-built bridge over the American River at Folsom, where they might pause to view the rapidly rushing waters of the American gushing out of its mountain canyon. Moving through Folsom, the motorist was asked to remember that Folsom was the head of navigation of the American River, the home of the

Improved roads provided Sacramentans with direct routes to favorite destinations. The Yolo Causeway, which opened in 1916, created a more direct route to the Bay Area and was a major breakthrough in the transportation history of the region.

county's electric generating plant, and also the famous state penitentiary. The return route took the tourist on through to Natomas, the headquarters of the Natomas Company, where its "great gold dredges are located," and past the piles and piles of rock where "dredges have turned up the soil in their quest for gold." Shuttling past olive orchards, vineyards, canning plants, small towns, and Mather Field, the auto ride eventually rejoined Folsom Boulevard and M Street through East Sacramento. Variations of the route were possible. "Most Sacramentans are familiar with the drive," said the *Bee.* However, "those who are not, those who have recently acquired cars or become residents in the city, as well as visitors, should take this trip some evening." Rail cars brought hundreds of automobiles to Sacramento in the 1920s and more and more Sacramentans found themselves behind the wheel.

The automobile allowed Sacramentans to travel the countryside as never before. Sunday and holiday trips became a part of family life.

Suburbanization

Automobile ownership also stimulated Sacramento's suburban development. North Sacramento became an automobile suburb (although it was connected with Sacramento by an electric train). Automobile traffic picked up steadily and North Sacramento's main commercial corridor, Del Paso Boulevard, hummed with traffic. Increasing numbers of autos were to be found along Folsom Road, Fair Oaks Boulevard, and Auburn Road, feeding the small "island" communities of Carmichael, Citrus Heights, Fair Oaks, and Orangevale. This laid the groundwork for the tremendous post–World War II suburban growth in those communities. The role of the automobile in the development of Oak Park, East Sacramento, and after 1923 the areas south of Y Street, was heralded by E. P. Huston, president of the Sacramento Realty Board, who observed in 1926, "Why without the automobile such sub-divisions as East Sacramento, Curtis Oaks, and dozens of others in this and other California cities would now be pasture land, worth perhaps a third of what it is at the present time."

The Auto and the Creation of Retail Districts

Automobile traffic helped to create new business districts around the state capital. In December 1925, plans were announced for a vast business district along Thirty-first Street (Alhambra Boulevard), stretching from J Street to M Street (Capitol Avenue), modeled after the Fillmore District in San Francisco. The district was to be an illuminated thoroughfare anchored by a new theater, the Alhambra, with stores, banks, and other retail outlets.

Auto dealers used free vacations as a marketing device as this Dodge-Plymouth dealer did in 1954.

Immediately to the south of the new theater, a 150-room motor hotel was planned in a Spanish motif, with an indoor court, a swimming pool, and a huge parking garage with individual spaces for 40 or 50 cars. It is interesting to note that one of the principal reasons the site was selected, according to a *Bee* reporter, "is because of an official check [showing] that 745,560 automobiles traveled Thirty-first Street in a period of thirty days." The number may have been an exaggeration, and in the end only the Alhambra Theater was built. However, several important auto dealerships opened up for business on this very busy street.

Automobile Dealership Districts

Sacramento's automobile dealerships have traditionally clustered in informal central locations. These locations have moved over the course of time. The first such district was along K Street between Twelfth and Sixteenth. However, the locales of auto dealerships began to change in the late 1920s as the city's residential districts moved east, south, and north. Studebaker dealer J. J. Jacobs announced plans in 1926 to erect a new building at Thirtieth and J in addition to his main dealership at Sixteenth and K. "Sacramento is growing so large," he stated, "and there is so much development in the residential districts that it becomes almost essential that a complete branch be maintained away from the business district. I believe that the trend of the automobile trade will find its expression in outer developments." Huge automobile showrooms and garages were built for the increasing number of auto dealers who needed extra space to house their inventories. A structure at Twelfth and H, owned by Cadillac dealer Don Lee, required a revision of the city's zoning ordinance to allow the structure to run to the middle of the block.

The increasing attention paid to the aesthetic features of garages and auto dealerships in the downtown was reflected in the magnificent Spanish-revival style building of the Arnold Brothers Hudson dealership. The building at Eighteenth and M (Capitol) opened to fanfare in 1924. It is today a popular restaurant (Zocalo's).

J. J. Jacobs (right) was one of the most prominent local auto dealers in the first half of the twentieth century. Second from right is Elmer Hubacher, an associate to whom Jacobs turned over his Cadillac dealership. Terry Fitzgerald and Dick Brown are on the left.

Auto Dealers in Sacramento History

J. J. Jacobs was one of the more memorable dealers of the early years of Sacramento auto retailing. Jacobs first became involved in the automobile business in New York City after answering an ad for a Ford salesman while he was selling typewriters in Montana. He enjoyed the car business and moved to Los Angeles in 1911. He took a brief sabbatical to be an extra in Hollywood, making films with Charlie Chaplin and Mack Sennett. After appearances in about 10 films and some other movie work, he resumed auto selling, hawking Studebakers in Los Angeles and Bakersfield. He then came to Sacramento to establish his own firm in 1916. In 1934, he took over distribution of Cadillacs, LaSalles, and Buicks. His first agency was at Eighteenth and M, and in 1917 he moved to Fifteenth and L. After General Motors stopped making LaSalles in 1941, he turned over his Buick agency to his son-in-law Newton Cope. Jacobs retired in 1966, and Elmer R. Hubacher, his partner and general manager since 1964, took over his Cadillac dealership.

E. A. Boyd was the owner of a local Chrysler-Plymouth dealership on the corner of Alhambra and L Street in 1936. Boyd was a friend of Walter P. Chrysler, the founder of the company, whom he had met when they worked together on the Southern Pacific Railroad. Ultimately, this firm sold out to J. R. Vandenberg, who became an important downtown Chrysler-Plymouth dealer. One of Boyd's early partners, Claude Coffing, was active in the city's expansion and growth and chaired an important postwar planning commission for the Chamber of Commerce. Coffing brought developer Jere Strizek to Sacramento, where he began a remarkable career as a home builder. Coffing had earlier been a partner to Royal Miller, who founded the city's first Dodge dealership in 1912. Miller was active in many aspects of Sacramento's civic life. In addition to founding radio station KROY and the

E. A. Boyd knew the legendary Walter Chrysler and sold his products in Sacramento for many years.

Royal Miller, a Dodge dealer, was active in a number of other local projects: radio, airlines, and banking. He also served on the Water Resources Board.

Capitol Air Lines (the first commercial firm to maintain scheduled flights from Sacramento), Miller was also a director of the Loyalty Savings and Loan and chairman of the California State Water Resources Board.

Postwar Automobility

Wartime shortages of steel, rubber, and gasoline slowed the pace of automobile sales and use in Sacramento. However, after the war Sacramentans resumed their love affair with the automobile. In 1953, 128,487 Sacramentans had cars—1 for every 2.1 persons in the county. The number of cars grew almost twice as fast as the county's population.

What was behind this explosive growth? Some of it was the purchase of huge fleets of automobiles for the needs of an expanding state government. However, the bulk of sales came from ordinary residents who simply needed transportation. Rusty Jacobs, a local dealer, summarized it best in 1963: "You can't live without them here. The suburbs are huge here and many workers have to come downtown to state offices—they have to have their own cars." Postwar Sacramentans, living in suburban areas, with no public transit, needed cars to get to their homes, shopping centers, recreational activities, churches, and social lives.

Every new suburban shopping center, school, and church had an ample parking lot. Suburban homes were built with driveways and at least a one-car garage—usually conveniently attached to the house. As adolescents obtained their drivers' licenses, the need for more than one family car became necessary.

But above all, cars took Sacramento suburbanites to work. McClellan Air Force Base, for a time the county's largest employer, had to continually widen Watt Avenue, the main access road to the installation. Mather Air Force Base, along with Aerojet and Douglas Aircraft, ensconced in the far eastern section of Sacramento County, required an expansion of State Highway 50—first to four lanes in 1957 and subsequently even wider—to accommodate the extra traffic coming its way.

More Road Building

Federal freeway construction began in earnest in the late 1950s. A 1949 survey of the state division of highways and the Federal Public Roads Administration revealed that nearly 350,000 automobile trips were generated daily in the Sacramento region totaling nearly one million vehicle miles, 84 percent of which were entirely within the county. Already in 1948, to satisfy those moving steadily northward and to end the congestion of the outer reaches of Twelfth Street to Auburn Road, the North Sacramento Freeway was built. A 1949 study called for the immediate construction of a bridge spanning the American River near Elvas, connecting Twentieth Street with the North Sacramento Freeway and Arden Way. This road, the shortest freeway in the world, opened in 1955.

The enactment of the Interstate Highway and Defense Act of 1956 inaugurated a program of public works roads unlike any in history. Sacramento was located along the route of Highway 40, one of the first paved national highways. The new interstate system extended Interstate 80, which ran from the Mississippi River to the west coast along a route that roughly paralleled the old transcontinental railroad. Interstate 80 went through the capital—cutting through its south side along the W to X Street neighborhoods. The section of Interstate 80 heading east toward Reno was rushed forward in order to provide better accessibility for the crowds attending the 1960 Winter Olympics at Squaw Valley. In the 1970s, Interstate 5 slashed through the city north and south.

The increased volume of automobile and truck traffic compelled a major rebuilding and expansion of historic Highway 99, which traversed the length of the Central Valley, in 1961. Highway 50 improvements also improved accessibility to Fair Oaks, Orangevale, and Folsom. These heretofore sleepy agricultural communities burst into life with subdivisions of ranch-style homes, two-car garages, and large driveways.

This is a view of westbound U.S. Highway 50 at the interchange of Highway 99 and the Capital City Freeway (I-80 Business).

The construction of the interstate system reworked the spatial and social geography of Sacramento. This photo of the W-X freeway taken in 1965 shows the path of this major transportation artery.

Highway 50 and the new Highway 99 took pressure off the heavily-traveled arterials of Stockton and Folsom Boulevards. But these freeways also gutted residential areas and commercial districts, changing the nature of neighborhoods. The alteration of traffic patterns sometimes meant the end of businesses, restaurants, and other commercial enterprises along what had once been heavily traveled roads. The city's long-serving streetcar system faded from the scene by the end of World War II, while the city's bus system remained afloat through public subsidies.

In the meantime, downtown Sacramento declined as the newly purchased automobiles and recently built freeways transported population into the suburbs. City officials in the late 1940s fretted that a lack of public parking and problems with traffic congestion were contributing to the decline of the central city. By 1949, local officials tagged the city's sluggish response to the traffic situation as its "number 1 problem" affecting the future of the Sacramento area. *Bee* reporter Bert Vaughn wrote ominously of the economic blight that hit cities lacking parking in downtown areas. "This can happen in Sacramento," he warned. The city created its system of one-way streets and widened or altered others (H and J Streets in particular) in order to make traffic flow more smoothly. Nearly 25 acres of right-of-way were secured between 1945 and 1948 for this purpose. To tackle the parking quandary, in 1950–1951 city officials approved the construction of a 1,400-space parking garage on an entire city block north of I Street and another on the block bordered by L and Capitol and Sixth and Seventh Streets. As noted, parking meters were introduced in 1945. Later, when downtown experienced a new burst of building in the 1980s, 1990s, and afterward, parking facilities were factored into construction plans.

The Relocation of Auto Row

Many auto dealers stayed at their familiar downtown locations in the old automobile row or along busily traveled Alhambra or Del Paso Boulevards. Still operating downtown during the postwar era was Burton Motors at Thirteenth and I Streets. At Thirteenth and K, Capitol Chevrolet still did business while rival Vogel Chevrolet remained at Sixteenth and I. Newton Cope sold Buicks at the corner of Fifteenth and K until he quit the business in 1959.

After the war, a major automobile center developed along Fulton Avenue in the northeast suburbs. A similar auto row evolved along Florin Road, one of the main commercial arteries on Sacramento's south side. Major auto dealerships also situated themselves along Madison Avenue, which ran

Capitol Chevrolet at 1300 K Street was a long-time downtown auto dealer.

through Carmichael, Citrus Heights, Fair Oaks, and Orangevale. Roseville in nearby Placer County, now a part of Sacramento's metropolitan region, had one of the first of these malls. Auto repair and service stations popped up everywhere near the subdivisions and shopping centers that developed in Sacramento.

One of the first dealers to locate along Fulton Avenue was Montana native Lew Williams, who sold Chevrolets. His dealership planted itself at the corner of El Camino and Fulton in 1955, just as the district was booming with the opening of Country Club Centre. By 1959, the street was full of auto dealers: Arden Plymouth Center, offering "the squarest deal in town" for its Plymouths and Valiants; Braley & Graham Buick; Country Club Motors, selling Lincoln, Mercury, and Continental models; International Sports Cars; and John E. Lukenbill's John's Motor Sales, which specialized in Volvo sales and service. By 1967, of the 35 dealers listed in the city directory, 10 were on Fulton Avenue and most of the rest were nearby. Newcomers by 1967 included Richard Niello Volkswagen and Mike Salta Pontiac. Fulton Avenue remains a major car selling zone in Sacramento. As dealerships evolved, good customer service, including service warranties for the upkeep and inevitable

Lew Williams Chevrolet Center was the anchor of the Fulton Avenue auto retail district. This photo was taken in 1956.

repairs, became part of the sales package. Thus, service departments evolved as another segment of the car lot and salesroom operations.

Florin Road, which exploded as a retailing avenue in the mid-1960s, soon became the locus of another major auto retailing operation. One of the first to land there was Dodge salesman Chuck Swift's dealership, which opened in the late 1960s—a year or so after the new Florin Center Mall debuted. Dealers were slow to follow Swift to Florin, but eventually expanding market possibilities convinced a number to open up in the south area. By 1981, in addition to Swift, Florin Toyota, River City Lincoln Mercury, and Senator Ford had outlets there. But changes were inevitable. Gene Pleau, a Ford dealer, summarized the major transition in auto retail locations in Sacramento: "When I first came here in 1963, there were 12 to 14 dealerships downtown. Today most dealers have migrated to the giant Roseville Auto Mall, the Folsom Auto Mall, and the Elk Grove Auto Mall. Fulton Avenue's auto row is about the same, but Florin Road and Madison Avenue have lost a few dealers."

What Did Sacramentans Buy

Sacramentans' taste in cars became more diverse over time. The appeal of luxury autos was limited, given the wage structure of most residents, but Cadillac dealers did a good business. Foreign car sales also began to pick up in the 1960s. Volkswagens, Porsches, BMWs, Volvos, and Saabs found a receptive Sacramento market in the 1960s and 1970s. More fuel efficient Japanese brands like Toyota, Datsun, and Honda began to pick up market share in the 1960s and gained even more sales after the oil crisis of 1973. In the early 1970s, three major Sacramento dealers reported booming sales: Florin Road Toyota, Turner Motors (Datsun), and Niello Volkswagen. In 1989, two of the three top sellers specialized in Japanese makes: Suburban Ford (marketing Ford, Daihatsu, and Isuzu); followed by Swift Dodge on Florin Road (selling Dodge, Jeep-Eagle, Rolls Royce, and Avanti); and Nissan (offering both Nissan and Subaru). In 1991 Swift Dodge claimed first place, but Florin Road Toyota had moved into third. In 2006, the top sellers were Roseville Toyota, John L. Sullivan Chevrolet, and Future Ford of Roseville.

The oil embargo of 1973 created shortages of gasoline all over the Sacramento area. This photo of a local Shell station shows the long lines. It also demonstrates how service stations had become self-service operations. The young woman in the foreground is offering free samples of a soft drink marketed by Anheuser-Busch. Mass consumption marketing strategies demonstrate that they can even use difficult circumstances to sell products.

Postwar Automobile Dealers

Two newcomers to the 1967 auto-dealer's network were Toyota of Sacramento and Swift Dodge on Florin Road. Texan Chuck Swift was one of Sacramento's great automobile entrepreneurs and one whose name was closely associated with a down-to-earth, friendly style of advertising that succeeded in bringing people to his lots. A native of Oglesby, Texas, Swift had begun his career in auto sales in Arizona. In 1967, he bought a Dodge dealership with his partner, Emmanuel Goldie, at Fifteenth and Broadway. A year later, he bought out Goldie and soon after moved the business to Florin Road. The highly successful Swift, a vigorous salesman, expanded his efforts to include a Mazda dealership, a car leasing operation (Swift Leasing), and a Rolls Royce franchise that he located on Fulton. In Davis, he purchased a dealership he had previously owned and operated, Swift

Jeep-Chrysler-Plymouth-Dodge. He even landed a contract to provide vehicles to the California Highway Patrol. Swift boosted his dealership to number one in northern California (primarily because of his fleet sales), and for a long time Swift Dodge was in the top 1 percent for sales among all Chrysler dealers in the nation. Swift himself became a Sacramento icon of sorts. Billing himself as "the little profit dealer," his gravelly voice was frequently heard on television spots. Swift's rapid delivery and quick wink became his trademarks. In a 1994 interview, Swift estimated that he had sold nearly 300,000 automobiles "so they would fit bumper to bumper to San Francisco and back."

One of Swift's rivals was Calvin Coolidge Worthington, a former daredevil flyer with a heroic military record. (He was a B-17 pilot with the 390th Bomber Squadron and flew 29 missions over Germany in World War II.) Worthington began his career selling used cars. In 1950 he owned a Hudson dealership in Los Angeles and then became involved in automobile retailing

The showroom of Capitol Chevrolet in 1956.

all over the West. He moved to Sacramento in 1981, establishing himself and his multiple dealerships with his flamboyant advertising. Appearing with a tiger or some other ferocious animal named "Spot" and wearing a white Stetson hat, Worthington presided over an automotive empire stretching from Alaska through California to Texas. The Worthington Dealership Group is headquartered at Worthington's 24,000-acre ranch, 90 miles north of Sacramento in Orland.

John L. Sullivan began auto retailing at his father's Kaiser-Nash dealership in San Bernardino in the early 1950s. In 1963 he came to Roseville and took a job as a used-car salesman for Ernie Caddell. He spent time working in Monterey and in a Volkswagen franchise owned by Paul Snider on Madison Avenue. He rejoined Caddell, bought out Caddell's partner in 1977, and in 1984 bought out Caddell. Under Sullivan, the Chevrolet dealership boomed, aided by the same kind of memorable advertising that worked well for Swift and Worthington. Sullivan engaged comedian Jim "Ernest" Varney to begin commercials with a folksy "Hey Vern!" Sullivan acquired Buick-Oldsmobile-Pontiac and GMC dealerships, and later a Volkswagen-Mazda-Isuzu dealership.

New dealers include a generation of owners' children who grew up learning the trade. Back in the 1950s, Wes Lasher and Richard Niello were partners in a Volkswagen dealership downtown. Following the population, Niello went to Sacramento's north area and Lasher went south. Lasher's sons, Mark and Scott, took over their father's business on Florin Road and in the Yolo County seat of Woodland. Niello's sons, Rick and Roger, head the Niello Company today. Randy Graham, son of the late Clark Graham, runs Braley & Graham GMC on Fulton. Mel Rapton, a longtime Honda dealer on Fulton, turned over the reins to his daughter Katrina and son Curtis. Bob Swift, son of Chuck Swift, is the general manager of Swift Auto World on Arden Way.

The collective forces of retail marketing dictated bigger, more centralized, more service-oriented facilities—one-stop shopping at a central location became an important feature in the evolution of marketing on every front—and this led to the emergence of the auto mall—a major center for mass consumption.

The Auto Mall

The enactment of Proposition 13, approved by voters in 1978, had an important effect on the placement of large retail outlets. This historic property tax limit law made local governments very dependent on sales taxes. As a result, localities now eagerly bid for big-box stores and automobile dealerships whose taxes replenished depleted public coffers.

Plans for an "auto mall"—a clustering of different dealerships all within an easily accessible location visible from the freeway, with plenty of room for customer and employee parking and service operations—had been tried in other parts of the country. The idea of such a mall in Placer County near the old railroad suburb of Roseville was first proposed in 1987. Developers predicted millions of dollars in increased tax revenues along with 1,000 new jobs to boost the local economy. Aggressively courted by Placer County officials, who helped with supporting infrastructure, the "Roseville Gang" chose an 87-acre parcel in the Olympus Pointe development, south of Interstate 80 between Atlantic Street and Douglas Boulevard. The new mall was announced in 1988 with 10 dealerships. "We believe the Roseville Auto Mall will represent the finest facilities in new car sales in Northern California, if not the whole state," predicted Chevrolet dealer John L. Sullivan.

High start-up costs and poor national economic conditions depressed hopes for the mall at first, but eventually it became what it had been predicted to be—a major outlet for the sale and service of automobiles in the Sacramento region. Another auto mall in Elk Grove developed in the 1990s, and soon surpassed sales expectations. After a setback, Folsom also put together a package of land and infrastructure improvements along Highway 50 to create an automobile retailing center. Auto malls do a brisk business. In 2005, of the 25 dealers on the *Sacramento Business Journal's* list of largest new car dealers, nine resided in auto malls. In 2006, the list included 11.

Sacramento itself vied to secure an auto mall along the Interstate 80 corridor. In April 2000 Mike Daugherty, who occupied the anchor Chevrolet-Hummer dealership on Fulton and El Camino, proposed the creation of an Autoplex just west of Northgate Boulevard with room for about a dozen dealerships. Daugherty offered to be the first to go out there and predicted revenues between $400 and $500 million with anywhere from $40 million to $50 million in tax revenue for the city. Daugherty purchased land in north Natomas and received permission from General Motors to move. In the meantime, big-box retailers such as Lowe's, Wal-Mart, and Home Depot were eyeing Daugherty's site. Ultimately plans for the deal fell through when Daugherty was unable to secure the necessary freeway access for his project. The city then bought the 25 acres from Daugherty for a reported $3.5 million.

County officials, fearful of losing tax revenue from the Arden-Arcade dealerships (totalling $7.3 million by 2006), worked hard to keep the Fulton dealers where they were. Fulton Avenue's auto row, which was home to 25 new car franchises, including a number of upscale vehicle dealers and even more used-car outlets, had been the main provider of tax revenue for the unincorporated Arden-Arcade area for years. These dealers banded together to resist additional competition and to upgrade their aging facilities. In March 2007, Sacramento County supervisors agreed to pay Mike Daugherty—still anxious for an "improved location"— $100,000 a year for 10 years to remain on his spot. The provisos that would stop the stipend: if Arden Arcade were to become a city or if Arden Arcade was annexed to Sacramento.

In June 2007, the Sacramento City Council approved a plan for Mel Rapton, a Fulton Avenue Honda dealership, to lease the former Sacramento Trapshooting Club property along the Capital City Freeway at the north end of Fulton in order to expand his business. The city will spend $9 million for cleanup of the property (17 of the 21 acres are contaminated with lead shot and clay pigeon remnants) and water drainage and electrical infrastructure, which it anticipates recovering within seven years.

Another shake-up for the Fulton auto row occurred in the fall of 2007, when Hubacher Cadillac decided to create a GM superstore on its 6.5 acre site at Howe Avenue and Fair Oaks Boulevard after the company purchased Randy Graham's General Motors dealership. Regarding the transaction and creation of the superstore, Hubacher's Brian Castonguay remarked on

As automobile ownership increased, service stations were strategically located all over the city. Note the attendants in uniforms. They not only pumped the gas, but also washed windshields. (Courtesy Sacramento Room, Sacramento Public Library.)

the need "for a location with the kind of design and style General Motors expects . . . and we want it to be well-received by the public."

Other automotive related businesses changed as well. Large chain repair shops such as Honest Engine and Jiffy Lube flourished with numerous branch outlets to take care of auto repair and maintenance—from tuneups to major engine rebuilding. Oil change and car wash facilities did a booming business as outlets also developed along main roads with easy in-and-out access. A visit to the state-of-the-art Harv's car wash on Seventeenth and L Streets provides an array of car cleaning services, all pushed through with assembly line efficiency.

Few service stations anywhere have the once friendly, uniformed auto attendant who pumped gas, washed the windshield, and checked the oil.

They have been replaced by self-service stations with credit card reading gas pumps. Many service stations are now mini-marts, carrying a small selection of groceries, drinks, candy, bagged ice, and lottery tickets.

Even though Sacramento has developed a very efficient and popular light rail system, and downtown workers are again snapping up homes and buying condominiums in the city, the region's devotion to the automobile remains undiminished.

3. "Push the Cart Around and 'Round"
Grocery Shopping

Sacramentans had to eat. While native peoples sustained themselves on the abundant acorns, game, fish, and roots of the area, American settlers brought other culinary tastes. Sutter's Fort was, among other things, a commissary for hungry travelers. Merchants opened shops at the fort and traded in staples, cured meats, and dried foods. Part of the success of gold-rush era Sacramento was the rapidity with which food merchants were able to respond to the deluge of miners who descended on the embarcadero as a way station to the mines. Miners could pick up, often at high price, coffee, salted pork or beef, crackers, and other victuals to sustain themselves in the gold fields. Restaurants also did a thriving business with foodstuffs grown nearby and also sent up from San Francisco. Local wheat, hops, oats, and other grains were sold in Sacramento and shipped elsewhere. As the community grew, an array of butchers, bakers, green grocers, and others arrived to meet the growing demand.

Early Food Merchants

Sacramento developed a wide array of grocery firms that received regular shipments from San Francisco suppliers via the river port and later by rail. Future governor Newton Booth began a retail grocery company in the 1850s on Front Street between J and K. With a wholesale house in San Francisco, Booth and his associates provided an assortment of goods to Sacramentans. Booth was not the only grocer who went into politics. Christopher Green, a native of Ireland, was one of the proprietors of the Empire Market, a meat and grocery firm. Green served two terms as Sacramento's mayor. Lindley & Company did business in Sacramento from 1869 to 1928. A wholesale tea importer and coffee roaster, this firm was identified with "Cherub Brand Foods" and the even more popular

This was a substantial newspaper ad for a locally roasted coffee.

Lindley's Motor Coffee—supposedly named thus because its high quality moved it rapidly from the grocer's shelf. This product was familiar to Sacramento coffee drinkers for many years. The Adams and McNeill Company, another wholesaler, was located in a large storehouse on Front Street. Its widespread territory extended into Oregon, Nevada, and Utah. They reported selling more than six million pounds of sugar and 80,000 pounds of cheese in 1876. G. W. Chesley, also on Front Street, specialized in wines and liquors, marketing Gilt Edge, Old Bourbon, various types of Kentucky whiskey, and later Budweiser beer.

Local ranchers, farmers, slaughter houses, and process plants provided beef, pork, and poultry to Sacramento residents. Meat markets served Sacramento customers well into the twentieth century. One highly visible firm was Mohr and Yoerk, located first on Tenth and J and later in a shop at Eleventh and K, across from the Cathedral of the Blessed Sacrament. Sacramentans could purchase hams, bacon, and lard under the "Our Taste" brand, distributed through the firm of Hall, Luhrs & Company. Father and son Charles and George Swanston operated another meat-packing firm on Riverside Road using one of Sacramento's first cold storage plants. George Swanston erected an even larger and more sophisticated packing facility in North Sacramento and operated it until 1948. Clauss & Kraus, located at Seventeenth and I Streets, was another memorable Sacramento meat-processing and retail firm. The C & K logo lasted into the 1980s as the firm continued to process meat and sell it to local stores.

In the early years, the products in these stores were often sold in bulk and not branded. Meats were cured, not fresh. Later, mass production techniques provided a new array of foods and packaging that revolutionized food distribution.

Interior of Clauss & Kraus Meat Market c. *1920. Meat cutters are behind counters, and meat hangs from hooks.*

Hog butchering and other meat processing industries were an important part of Sacramento's local food provision operations.

Producing, Processing, Packaging: A Revolution in Food Supply

Important technological changes in the late nineteenth and early twentieth centuries transformed the production of food and its marketing in America. First, the amount of food grown in America increased substantially. The advent of scientific farming methods produced hybrids of fruits, vegetables, and grains for the American table. Advances in animal husbandry and changes in the raising of livestock created more and more food on the hoof. The Sacramento Valley federal and state land reclamation and irrigation policies put even more land under cultivation. Improvements in fertilization, cultivation, pest control, and new agricultural machinery made it possible for fewer and fewer farmers to produce more and more food. By the early twentieth century, America was swimming in agricultural surpluses. Sacramentans had only to travel a few miles up the valley to see these developments with their own eyes.

Food scientists and others who studied the microbiological and chemical makeup of food devised techniques to improve food processing and preservation. Louis Pasteur's efforts to end the spoilage of wine and milk significantly advanced the safety of the food supply. Pasteurization and other sanitary precautions, especially those mandated by the federal government in the Pure Food and Drug Act and the Meat Inspection Act of 1906, made the food supply even more reliable. Technological innovations in refrigeration advanced steadily in the twentieth century as old ice boxes gave way to continually chilled refrigerator cabinets and walk-in coolers and freezers. The large-scale production of refrigerators for commercial and home use had a significant impact on food marketing practices.

Just as important were developments in food freezing. These are often attributed to Clarence Birdseye, who first patented this form of food preservation in the 1930s. The Postum Company (later General Foods) acquired Birdseye's patents. Birdseye sold packaged meat, fish, vegetables, and fruit from low-temperature display cases that soon became standard fixtures in American markets. Other innovations included fruit juice concentrates packaged in tube-shaped cans, and new kinds of sweeteners. The mass production of baking powder effected a mini-revolution in the development of commercially-produced baked goods. Sacramento developed its own bread factories, which marketed the popular Betsy Ross bread and later Blue Seal brands. Wonder Bread is still made in the state capital. Food processing firms like General Foods, Nabisco, Kraft Foods, Armour, and Swift, as well as major canning companies (some of which were in Sacramento), adapted these new technologies on a large scale.

Food companies created new forms of packaging that allowed goods to be shipped farther. They also "branded" their products to make them more appealing to consumers. In 1898 Adolphus Green developed a flakier and more crisp cracker that was wrapped in an individual "sanitary" package and sold in a box. U-Needa Biscuits, one of the first of many packaged products from the National Biscuit Company (Nabisco), were an instant success. These crackers are often heralded as the beginning of a trend in food processing and purchasing. Kellogg's Cereal company in Battle Creek, Michigan, is credited with putting breakfast cereal in cardboard boxes. Branded on the outside with attractive lettering and logos, packaged products soon began to replace the open sacks of grain and cereals, just as U-Needa Biscuits replaced the old cracker barrel. Maxwell House coffee, first offered to guests at the

Schaden's Grocery (above) and the Enos Brothers store (below) are examples of how groceries were sold prior to self-service innovations.

Maxwell House Hotel in Nashville, Tennessee in 1892, became one of the first coffee products marketed in easy-to-open cans.

The explosive growth in food supply coupled with innovative marketing techniques transformed the food industry. Large wholesale purchasing became a necessity to sell food in the volume necessary to make a profit. New kinds of food retailing strategies developed in order to accommodate the growing demand for these products.

Grocery stores of the early twentieth century ended the old system whereby clerks picked and selected store items for a customer or bagged bulk products such as flour, oats, rice, and dry legumes. Soon to follow, produce, meat, and bakery goods, which had been sold in separate operations, came under the aegis of one marketplace.

New grocery stores created wide-open shelves where customers could make their own selections of the packaged and branded products. Grocery carts were eventually provided for convenient self-service shopping. These carts grew ever larger and eventually even included a space to carry an infant or toddler. At the end of the shopping trip, customers "checked out" with a clerk who tallied the prices at a centralized location. Bag clerks completed the transaction.

Adequate wholesale facilities and the intense competition for customers pushed ambitious grocers to operate multiple stores, strategically located in growing neighborhoods. Successful grocers expanded their operations into chain stores to increase their market share and profits. At the same time, they offered a much greater array of products and services to generate higher sales volume. The new supermarkets were surrounded by capacious parking lots. Chain markets advertised heavily, and used a variety of methods to encourage shopper loyalty (discounts, stamps, and give-away promotions of every type).

The Arata Brothers

The Arata brothers claim pride of place in any history of Sacramento grocery retailing. Charles, Frank, and Andrew Arata hailed from Jackson in Amador County, where Andrew ran a grocery store that catered to

The Arata Brothers helped to transform the way food was sold in the city of Sacramento.

miners. In 1908 the brothers opened a grocery store at Eleventh and J Streets that stocked groceries, liquor, produce, and even hardware. By 1916 they had a branch store in Oak Park on Sacramento Avenue and by 1930 four others. The brothers worked hard and were remembered later by another grocer as "the most progressive and aggressive grocers of the time." Initially retailers, they soon expanded their stores or "groceterias" to various locations in Sacramento and eventually built a large warehouse at Thirty-third and Broadway in Oak Park to store wholesale goods. The creation of wholesale warehouses was indispensable for the high-volume trade that chain stores and later supermarkets were undertaking. Quantity buying of grocery products meant a lower per-unit cost, which could be passed on to consumers—an indispensable advantage in the highly-competitive grocery business. Chains from outside the region often had greater buying power, because they were big enough to have their own warehouses. Other smaller chains organized the United Grocers Association and operated their own local warehouses. An independent grocer's association (IGA) also formed. Even some of the old-time grocers—Mebius-Drescher, Hall, Luhrs & Co., Lindley & Company, and Bert McDowell—in a valiant effort to compete with the new chain stores, had attempted to form their own wholesale operation in 1925.

The Aratas carved an important niche for their wholesale business through the marketing of produce. Taking advantage of the variety of fruits and vegetables in the fields, orchards, and truck farms of Sacramento's hinterlands, Charles Arata worked closely with local farmers to procure fresh produce, which he sold to small grocers. The Arata warehouse did an enormous business and was one of the largest-volume operations in northern California.

The Aratas advertised regularly in the Sacramento dailies, and even took out double-truck ads (two consecutive pages) in the *Sacramento Bee* as early as 1932. It is possible the Arata brothers introduced self-service grocery shopping to Sacramento, or perhaps picked up the technique from another chain store that moved into Sacramento at about the time they were beginning to expand. As with so many other food retailers in Sacramento, the Arata Brothers chain passed into history, unable to keep up with the fast-paced changes demanded by the retail grocery industry. The stores eventually closed, and the wholesale warehouse folded shortly after the death of Andrew Arata in 1962. In 1968, the building was sold to a Reno firm and eventually became the home of the Sacramento Food Bank, a local charity.

Piggly Wiggly and Safeway: The Chain Store Comes to Sacramento

The first national chain to come to Sacramento was the "daddy" of American self-serve markets, Piggly Wiggly. Founded in Memphis, Tennessee in 1916 by Clarence Saunders, the chain pioneered the self-service concept. Everyone had a cart to push through the aisles of open shelves in the various departments. All brand names were carefully tagged so shoppers would know the cost. "Come in now," one ad beckoned, "and get acquainted with a system of Scientific Merchandising." Another ad said, "Select with your own hands exactly what you want. Have a delightful Easter dinner and know that it has cost you less than if there were no Piggly Wiggly stores." Piggly Wiggly brought this format to Sacramento on April 29, 1921, when it began operations on the downstairs floor of the Weinstock, Lubin & Co. store. (Interestingly, Hale's department store also hosted a groceteria in its lower level for several years.) Each first-day visitor of a new Piggly Wiggly received a fresh carnation as he or she walked in the door. The Weinstock location did not last long, but by 1928 the aggressive chain had opened in seven locations mostly in the downtown area, but also on Thirty-fifth Street and another on Stockton Boulevard. Saunders eventually lost control of the company in the late 1920s, and Piggly Wiggly disappeared from the Sacramento scene. Other chain groceries opened branches in Sacramento: Martha

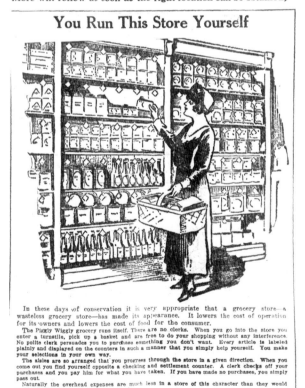

More will follow as soon as the right location can be obtained)

You Run This Store Yourself

In these days of conservation it is very appropriate that a grocery store—a wasteless grocery store—has made its appearance. It lowers the cost of operation for its owners and lowers the cost of food for the consumer.

The Piggly Wiggly grocery runs itself. There are no clerks. When you go into the store you enter a turnstile, pick up a basket and are free to do your shopping without any interference. No polite clerk persuades you to purchase something you don't want. Every article is labeled plainly and displayed on the counters in such a manner that you simply help yourself. You make your selections in your own way.

The aisles are so arranged that you progress through the store in a given direction. When you come out you find yourself opposite a checking and settlement counter. A clerk checks off your purchases and you pay him for what you have taken. If you have made no purchases, you simply pass out.

Naturally the overhead expenses are much less in a store of this character than they would be if a staff of clerks was kept in attendance.

The waste is much less than it is in the average grocery store. In weighing food hurriedly there is often a little of the substance being weighed, as well as the danger of the weight being over or under the desired amount. When the material is weighed without hurry or anxiety, the results are more satisfactory.

This Piggly Wiggly ad demonstrated the wonders of self-service grocery stores.

Safeway stores are important contributors to grocery retailing in Sacramento. This 1955 photograph shows a new store with a capacious parking lot.

Washington, Skaggs Cash Stores, and Economic Food Co. All of them used the modern self-serve format.

Safeway was another outside firm that established strong Sacramento roots. Begun in 1914 in southern California, Safeway was the creation of a major consolidation of competing businesses. Prior to coming to Sacramento, the firm at first confined its California operations to Los Angeles, San Diego, and Bakersfield. One of its mergers was, however, with the Skaggs Company, which had four retail outlets in Sacramento. In November 1926 Sacramentans heard of the merger, which created a veritable grocery empire in the West consisting of 784 retail grocery stores, 122 meat markets, and six bakeries. The number of Safeway outlets in Sacramento steadily increased, including stores in what were then outlying districts south along Broadway, east of Alhambra, and along Highway 99 and Folsom Boulevard. By 1932, there were 19 Safeways operating in Sacramento.

Other locally-based chain stores appeared with increasing frequency in the 1920s, 1930s, and 1940s. Cardinal stores began in 1927. By 1932, Cardinal Grocery had nine locations in the Sacramento area. Thomas Porter Raley, destined to become the giant of Sacramento area retail grocers, came

The Cardinal stores had a long run of success in the Sacramento area. The Food Depot was at 1120 H Street.

to California from Arkansas in 1925. After a stint in the grocery business in the Bay Area, he moved to Placerville in 1935 and opened a small store. In 1938, he commenced operations in Sacramento with a store on Stockton Boulevard. Although he later sold this property, he branched out in all directions. Raley proved to be a genius in selecting locations for his growing chain and also for keeping up with the changing developments in marketing. His legacy left his daughter, Joyce Raley Teel, sole owner of the eighth largest privately-held company in California. Forbes ranked her as the fifth wealthiest businesswoman in the United States, with an estimated worth of $1.1 billion in 2006.

Some of the chain-store grocers in Sacramento began as small mom-and-pop operations. Such was the case with the Kassis brothers, a Lebanese family who had come to Sacramento in the 1920s from North Dakota. Under the leadership of the family patriarch A. G. Kassis, the sons began a successful business with a fruit stand on Twenty-eighth and Broadway (Y Street). Hardworking, close-knit, and endowed with a keen business sense, these brothers soon learned the principles of the modern supermarket, christening their enterprise Stop 'n Shop. They leveraged the profits from their stores into acquiring additional facilities. Eventually they had a chain of 12 grocery stores scattered all over the Sacramento area. Stop 'n Shop, like most grocery chains, advertised primarily through the newspapers. However, the chain also gave Sacramento one of its most memorable radio and television ad jingles, composed by a writer at radio station KRAK:

> Let's go down to the Stop 'n Shop
> And Push the Cart Around and 'Round
> You get a lot more for your dollar there
> Than anywhere else in town!

The Public Market

One idea that would catch on all over the country was the concept of a central marketplace, where independent purveyors could set up shop and market their goods. The central market would provide storage,

The Public Market on Thirteenth and J Streets hosted a number of different food sellers under one roof. This anniversary sale article lists ten separate operations.

cooling units, and open space to sell perishables. Sacramento's Public Market brought this concept to the state capital when it opened its doors in 1924. The idea apparently had been suggested to Lizzie Glide of Berkeley, a widow with a fortune in Kern County oil. On a visit to Glide in November 1922, A. R. Gallaway of the Wright & Kimbrough real estate agency proposed that she underwrite the building of a public market, which would house competitive tenants selling a variety of food products. Glide launched her own investigation of similar entities in other regions of the country and concluded that it could be a successful venture. She engaged architect Julia Morgan to design a sturdy building on the corner of Thirteenth and J, replete with brick facing, terra cotta, and black marble trimmings. State-of-the-art refrigeration, hydraulic elevators to move stock from the basement, and adequate lighting were integrated into the building, with its large, open lower floor and balcony/mezzanine section. The store had a gala opening in November 1923 that included a 10-piece orchestra. It touted 24 vendors that included meat shops, a creamery, condiments, coffee, and at least four fresh and dried fruit and vegetable stands. There was even a branch of the Piggly-Wiggly chain. Manager Henry Glide, Lizzie's son, extolled the centralization of food distribution, cooperative and centralized buying, and the importance of sanitary facilities for the preparation and preservation of food. While purveyors came and went over the years, the Public Market continued to do business until the 1970s. Its Julia Morgan façade was preserved as an architectural treasure of the city, and it currently welcomes guests to the Sheraton Grand Hotel, which now occupies the space.

The Beavis Meat Company was one of the purveyors at the Public Market.

The Supermarket Concept

As Henry Glide was praising the virtues of "centralization" at the Public Market, important changes in food retailing continued to take place. One of the most important vehicles in the mass production food market was the advent of the "super" market. Supermarkets brought all types of food-selling operations—meat, dairy products, produce, packaged goods, and household items—under one roof and laid them out in sections or departments of the stores, staffed by clerks who replenished the supplies. The origins of the modern supermarket—a huge warehouse-type building with multiple departments, low-prices, self-service, central checkout, and flamboyant advertising—can be traced to several sources. Some historians cite Michael Cullen of Jamaica, New York, who opened a "warehouse grocery" (King Cullen—reminiscent of King Kong) in a former garage on Long Island. Others point to similar developments made by Ralph's Grocery Company, a longtime Los Angeles firm that began as a typical clerk service and delivery operation, but which also used large warehouse buildings for marketing groceries. The supermarket had no frills, made its profits on volume trade, and utilized bold advertising to bring in customers. Other innovations like self-service, accommodations for automobiles, and the convenience of one-stop shopping made these large super markets the standard for grocery marketing. According to historian Alfred Yee, the term "supermarket" was coined by William H. Albers, who was the first to give his store this now-familiar sobriquet in 1933. By 1955, supermarkets sold 60 percent of groceries to American consumers. It was the vehicle of mass consumption par excellence.

Chain Stores Evolve into Supermarkets

When did the supermarket concept first come to Sacramento? It's hard to say. Eventually, chain grocery companies that survived the intense competition remodeled their stores into supermarkets. This certainly happened with the host of local chain store operations, including Arata Brothers, Cardinal,

The Lucky's supermarket chain first came to Sacramento in 1948. Lucky stores, like this one built in 1955, stretched out over the entire metropolitan area.

Inks Brothers, Stop 'n Shop, and Raley's. One outside firm that surged ahead was the Lucky chain. Begun in 1935 by investor Charles Crouch in the Bay Area, Lucky's gave stiff competition to rival Safeway in Oakland and other East Bay locations. Lucky's opened its first supermarket in San Leandro in 1947. Its initial store in Sacramento opened on Thirtieth and Broadway in 1948. In 1955, Lucky opened an 18,000 square-foot market on Fruitridge Road and a 15,000 square-foot market in North Highlands. In 1956, Lucky's took over some of the old Cardinal stores and substantially expanded its presence in the area.

Cardinal stores also provided the nucleus for the Inks brothers, who developed a thriving supermarket chain for awhile. The brothers—Charles, Russell, and Dick—originally began their chain-store work with Cardinal stores in 1927. Russell and Dick Inks left the firm in 1940 and in 1941 opened up their own Inks Brothers market on Sacramento Boulevard. From this store, the Inks retail empire eventually grew to 16 Sacramento area locations. In January 1952, they too picked up the pieces of the now

Cardinal-Inks stores did very well in suburbs like North Highlands. This 1952 ad shows the use of trading stamps—a popular marketing tool for shoppers who saved them for various household products.

fading Cardinal chain and reunited with their brother Charles to form the Cardinal-Inks stores. This created a network of 33 supermarkets, 29 of them in the Sacramento area. The Inks brothers moved confidently into the rapidly developing suburbs. In 1953 the brothers secured a prime four-acre site on North A Street in the burgeoning suburb of North Highlands, where they built the major grocery outlet of the area. By 1959, the store could brag that it sold more of the four major brands of beer than any other retail outlet in northern California. That store also tallied the largest gross receipts of the Sacramento chain. A similar opening at the rapidly expanding Fruitridge Shopping Center on Stockton Boulevard also did a handsome business.

The Kassis brothers remade their network of stores into modern supermarkets. A 1951 company profile highlighted the evolution of the "many services under one roof" philosophy. At the store on Riverside Boulevard, which they opened in 1947, the brothers hosted complete grocery, produce, and meat departments, as well as a home appliance shop, barber and hairdressing shops, dry cleaners, post office, bakery, drugstore, and gift shops—all under one roof. In many of their stores, the brothers experimented with different floor layouts and expanded on a concept called "concourse merchandising," which they had effectively used at their Riverside location. At a new store on Twenty-eighth and L, they entered into an association with Hart's Pastry and the popular confectioner See's Candy. In 1982, Sutter Hospital purchased the site for its new hospital. As the Kassis brothers reached the apogee of their supermarket chain with 12 profitable stores around Sacramento, they threw their collective energy and accumulated business wisdom into the development of the Arden Fair shopping center.

The Kassis family, major grocery store entrepreneurs, are pictured here at the opening of their new Riverside store. Neon signs indicate the availability of Green Stamps and a pharmacy. From left to right are Fred David (owner of the Solons), Maggie Kassis (mother), Walter, John, Muriel, Frank, Bill, and Lewis. (Courtesy Kassis family.)

Jumbo Market, one of several successful chains run by Chinese grocers. This 1979 store was in Granite Bay Shopping Village at Douglas Boulevard and Auburn Folsom Road.

Chinese merchants also played an important role in the diffusion of supermarkets around Sacramento. Chinese retailers included Famous Foods, Farmers, Jumbo, Parade, Giant, and other independent retailers who carved out niches in the expanding city. Relying on family ties and reduced labor costs, Chinese markets thrived for a time on the Sacramento supermarket scene. Perhaps the most famous Chinese-run market was Bel Air, founded by the Wong family. Gim and Lee Shee Wong had immigrated from China in 1922 and purchased acreage in the Auburn area of Placer County to grow fruits and vegetables. They eventually bought a small store in Penryn and sold produce door-to-door. Six Wong children helped the family business. The eldest, Bill Wong, recalled, "I started my own store in 1947 at Twenty-eighth and P." A stint in the army during the Korean War interrupted his career. In 1955, his family pooled its resources and opened the first Bel Air market at Sixty-third and Fruitridge, naming it for the posh Los Angeles suburb. By 1989, Bel Air had 13 stores in the Sacramento area and held an enviable 12.5 percent of the area's grocery business—exceeded only by Lucky's and Raley's. Bel Air stores would be among the first to introduce electronic scanners to record food purchases, beginning with the Elk Grove store in 1977. In 1992, Raley's Corporation acquired the chain.

The supermarket was above all an important part of the suburban expansion of the Sacramento area. As early as the 1920s, the demands of automobile owners for adequate parking elicited a response from grocers. For example, the Arata brothers move from their original Eleventh and J location to a new facility at Sixteenth and S for "better parking facilities and lower rents." In 1935, a Park 'n Shop opened on Folsom Boulevard, which had a small parking lot. Chain stores followed the expanding population of the Sacramento area. Developers, especially in the postwar era, often built large shopping centers in the heart of booming subdivisions. Supermarkets were the anchors that attracted other stores—druggists, florists, tailors, dry cleaners, and such—to locate there as well. These shopping centers included ample parking lots for suburban motorists.

Merger Mania

The late twentieth century was even more fast-paced and competitive for supermarkets. Alfred Yee observed that to survive, stronger supermarkets bought out the weak ones so they could increase their own market share. This spared them the start-up expense of opening new stores. Thus, a bewildering array of mergers and consolidations took place, leaving a diverse food retailing industry in Sacramento. Older Sacramento chains like Stop 'n Shop and Inks Brothers, as well as other chains like Van's Markets, simply could not keep up with the ever-growing mega-supermarkets that the new era produced. Supermarket innovations popped like firecrackers as chains installed new and more appealing layouts, expanded produce sections, and responded to changes in food consumption, especially health and gourmet foods. Stores continually upgraded their services and their selection, including popular take-out like Chinese, salads, sandwiches, and other ready-to-eat foods, to appeal to lunch and dinner crowds anxious to avoid waits at restaurants and fast-food establishments.

By the 1950s, Thomas Raley had begun his steady ascent as one of Sacramento's leading grocery retailers. In 1953 he had a small chain of seven stores in the Sacramento area, including sites in newly developing areas along Freeport Boulevard, Sutterville Road, and Fruitridge Road. The number of stores began to expand and their size kept up with the increasing volume of shoppers. In 1973, Raley's opened their first mega-market. Working hard to maintain a competitive edge, Raley's and its competitors pooled resources to bring down wholesale prices by building large warehouses. Bel Air and Modesto-based Save-Mart teamed with Raley to improve dairy prices. In the early 1980s, they curtailed their orders with the Crystal Cream & Butter Co. when they opened their own joint venture, Mid-Valley Dairy. In 1991, Raley's teamed up with the same group to build a huge wholesale warehouse called Westpac Pacific Foods. By this time, these three companies made up about 24 percent of northern California's grocery industry. Supermarket competition grew intense. Raley's, Lucky's, and Safeway battled each other for market share. In 1992 Raley's dominated area grocery retailing when it bought out the Wong family's Bel Air stores, already well known for their excellent service and upscale product line. This gave the company an impressive

Thomas Porter Raley (center) is pictured here in front of a new store in Carmichael.

37 percent of the Sacramento market in 1993. Raley's also bought out the Nob Hill Food Stores in San Francisco in 1998, a market it had been anxious to enter for many years. Lucky's, Raley's major competitor, went out of existence in 1999 when Albertsons, a chain based in Boise, Idaho purchased it. Farmers Markets, once with 25 stores in California, soon dropped to five with only one in Sacramento before it went bankrupt in 1984. The Chinese markets, which had depended for years on lower labor costs, were eventually compelled to unionize their workers. This erased their competitive edge in the very tight Sacramento market.

Sometimes stores competed against themselves. Safeway opened a low-cost food warehouse called Pak 'n Save, which eliminated baggers and other labor "overhead" in order to offer lower prices.

Ethnic and Small Markets

Although the huge supermarket chains dominated the mass consumption of food in Sacramento, other outlets continued to thrive in specialized markets. Ethnic markets led the way. Italians were a very large sub-group of the city population, and Italian groceries like the nineteenth-century retailer DeBenardis no doubt catered to their needs with various imported cheeses, wines, and pastas. Arata Brothers, Italian in origin, also had a share of the market. Sacramento had a respectable array of Italian stores, including Meda Brothers, Progress Importing Grocery (in the Public Market, later bought by the Pennisi family), the Jenovino Brothers at Twenty-sixth and J, and the Mazzuchi Brothers. The Corti Brothers were also part of this tradition.

Frank Corti had worked for Safeway as a manager for six years. In 1939, he was working for Best Foods when the chain sent him to Sacramento as a supervisor. He continued to work for Best in Sacramento for another six years. After World War II, he and his brother Gino, also with a background in the grocery business, decided to plunge into the speciality store business. In 1947 they purchased a store from Meda Brothers at Eighth and I, the old city morgue. When the block holding their store was purchased, they relocated in 1949 to a former Arata Brothers property at Thirty-second

Frank and Gino Corti, pictured here with family, launched a successful specialty store operation that at one time had several different chain stores. Today, the store at Fifty-ninth Street and Folsom Boulevard is still quite popular.

and Folsom Boulevard. The store soon began a popular catering service, specializing in meats, cheeses, pasta, olive oil, and other Italian specialty products. They expanded the store in the 1970s and began to open branches in various locations around the Sacramento metropolitan area, including Arden Fair Mall and Birdcage Walk (Citrus Heights). Their flagship store was on Thirty-fifth Avenue and Freeport Boulevard, anchoring a shopping center they bought and renamed the Cort Yard. The Corti Brothers stores had a reputation for specialty provisions advanced by Darrell Corti, who was an internationally-recognized wine and olive oil expert. David Berkeley, who was employed by Corti Brothers, became a local institution in his own right. He was the wine steward to Governor Ronald Reagan, and later to the Reagan White House, eventually opening his own establishment, David Berkeley Fine Wines and Specialty Food, at the upscale Pavilions Shopping Center in 1985.

Nevertheless, the heavy debt from the Corti's expansions, plus serious competition from supermarket chains that had installed their own delicatessens, led to the steady closing of the Corti stores, leaving only the one at 59th Street and Folsom Boulevard. Corti bought this location from Giant Foods, which had purchased it from Grand View Market.

Mexican markets existed in the Latino areas of South Sacramento, featuring an array of products used in Mexican cuisine. East West Foods at Forty-seventh Avenue and Forty-fourth Street imported products for Sacramento Muslims who hailed from Pakistan, Malaysia, Kenya, and India. Refusing to sell alcohol and "publications of questionable taste," the store also stocked meat that followed the religiously sensitive preparation processes specified in Muslim tradition and by the dictates of the Koran.

Even in the age of the mega market, Sacramento continues to have a wide variety of small corner grocery and specialty stores, especially in the midtown and Land Park areas. Many of these stores accommodate local residents, who frequent them for small items or drinks. Some, like Fremont Market at Twenty-fourth and N, survive on the sandwich-and-salad lunch trade. Chain convenience stores are located all over the Sacramento area. Self-service gasoline stations also sell hot and cold food items and drinks.

One older chain that still maintains its place is Compton's Market, which continues to survive along with the smaller, more efficient in-and-out groceries. Billy Joe "Bill" Compton, a native of Texas and Oklahoma, was an Air Force veteran who returned to Sacramento after being stationed here for two years. He worked for a time as a clerk in the Cardinal stores, and when Cardinal was bought out by Lucky's, Compton remained as a manager. Lucky invited managers to buy some of its smaller outlets, so Compton and his brother Lewis purchased a store on Stockton Boulevard near Fourteenth Avenue in 1957. Joined by another brother, Loy Compton, the family continued buying small stores. At its peak, the Compton chain had 13 locations in Sacramento County. By the middle of the 1980s, Compton's could no longer keep up with the competition, and the once-thriving chain of convenience stores was reduced to one on McKinley Boulevard in East Sacramento.

Taylor's Market on Freeport Boulevard sports an excellent produce, meat, and fresh bread concession, and is popular among Land Park and Curtis Park professionals who stop there on their way home from work to pick up fresh dinner items. Sacramento's Natural Foods Co-op on Alhambra and S specializes in organic foods and other specialty items desired by health-conscious Sacramentans.

The agencies of mass consumption only appear to operate independently from one another. In fact, automobile dealerships, grocery stores, housing, and other retail outlets are all interdependent. Grocery stores were built near residential areas, and the kinds of houses and neighborhoods that Sacramentans have occupied over the years is another piece of the larger picture of mass consumption.

4. "Preeminently a City of Homes"
Housing

Housing is generally the largest single expenditure that families or individuals make. This was true even in the late nineteenth century when the *Sacramento Bee* ran a series of articles on an array of elegant homes in the downtown area: "Sacramento is pre-eminently a city of homes . . . the man who owns his own home is a king. . . . Sacramento has many kings among her citizens." Sacramento prided itself on the number of homes in the city. On the eve of the Great Depression, the *Bee* bragged, "A large proportion of the area within the Sacramento City limits is devoted to home usage." Residential development (single-family dwellings, duplexes, and apartments) "occupies 73 percent of the city's total development area."

Decent wages and reasonable building costs allowed Sacramento to become a city of homeowners. There is even today an amazing variety of homes in the city. The ubiquitous Delta homes, set high above the ground to help residents avoid flood damage, remain prominent downtown. The city still has a spectacular assortment of Victorians. Although much reduced in number, they once dominated the area from Ninth and E to Tenth and H Streets. *Vanishing Victorians*, a popular guide to these architectural gems, notes that the elegant Albert Gallatin mansion, the former governor's residence, was "the anchor for a neighborhood of gracious homes from 14th to 18th."

The city basked in the sobriquet "Sacramento: City of Homes," using it frequently as a bragging point in boosterism. In the history of the city, real-estate brokers, land speculators, and home builders played an important part in growth and development. Charles Wright and Howard Kimbrough, J. C. Carly, Valentine McClatchy, Edward Alsip, and others bought and developed land and did everything they could to make it attractive for home builders and buyers. Early developers like Frank A. Williams, Charles Bell, Charles E. DeCuir, and Carroll Brock not only built residences, but named streets, created traffic control systems, and sold land for schools, parks, and churches. Although road and infrastructure improvements were sometimes painfully slow, the city planted rows and rows of leafy green trees along its streets, which among other things enhanced the neighborhood appeal of the city. Individual builders custom built most of the city's early homes. After World War II, the production of inexpensive housing and the world of easy credit created a major boom in home building and buying.

Sometime before World War I, the *Sacramento Bee* began a weekly development section highlighting major new buildings like the Elks Temple, Memorial Auditorium, and Alhambra Theater. It also reported the improvement of lands slated for residential use. The installation of electroliers (ornate street lamps), paved streets, sidewalks, and trees encouraged buyers to purchase lots and build homes. Home building jumped dramatically in the 1920s as better wages and more affordable homes in the developing areas north and south of the city took off.

The joy of home ownership opened to a wider and wider array of Sacramentans of every class. In 1925, E. P. Huston observed: "The owning

This three-story Victorian home is on H Street.

This home belonged to long-time Lutheran pastor, Reverend Charles Oehler.

of your own home idea is strong among the working class of Sacramento. . . . [they are] demanding an averaged price house of about $5,000." Chris Jones, a local land developer, noted improvements in design: "The tendency now is toward better class things and these are necessarily being supplied at lower costs. . . . One of these ordinary bungalows would have put to shame the finest palaces of a medieval prince. . . . People now want more than just a place to live; they want real homes."

Sacramento Expands

Early Sacramento homes were custom built for individual buyers, and the districts where they were located became increasingly more defined. Historian Amanda Paige Meeker notes that downtown remained a popular residential district until the early twentieth century, with Victorian and Delta homes near the state capitol between Tenth and Fifteenth, and K and O Streets. As this area was transformed into a business and rental property district, home building stretched out in every direction. Eventually residential boundaries

These two Sacramento Bee ads extolled the virtues of home ownership but also offered practical tips on how to buy a home.

pushed beyond the Eighteenth Street limit, and a "homes" section, east of Eighteenth, sprouted a number of different custom built homes of various designs and sizes. To the south of R Street, real estate speculators like County Supervisor Robert Callahan pushed Sacramentans to build homes in the vicinity of Southside Park.

To the southeast of the city limits, developers like Edward Alsip planned Oak Park, the city's first streetcar suburb. With the addition of streetcar service to the area, Alsip began to divide the area into small lots on which a variety of homes were built. According to local historian Lawrence Adams, Oak Park's housing reflected the income levels of its inhabitants. Well-to-do professionals who came to the suburb sometimes built high-priced Queen Anne–style homes. Oak Park was ultimately annexed to the city in 1911.

East Sacramento

"The trend of residential expansion is moving eastward and southward . . . as new city tracts are opened and new homes spring up with great rapidity," noted the *Bee* in 1925. East Sacramento's Tract 24, a 146-acre parcel running from Fortieth to Forty-seventh Streets and J Street to Folsom Boulevard, would become well known for its upscale homes. Locals referred to the tract as the "Fabulous Forties." The land had once been owned by physician Gregory Phelan. His widow eventually sold it to developer Charles Wright and his partner Howard Kimbrough, two of Sacramento's most energetic twentieth century real-estate developers. Eventually P. G. & E. extended streetcar service along J Street, which unlocked the development potential of this area. Wright & Kimbrough divided Tract 24 into lots bigger than those downtown. Along streets originally named for some of Sacramento's leading businessmen, like Breuner, Steffen, McClatchy, and Yardley, the company graded and paved, put in sidewalks and a sewer system, planted trees, and installed electroliers. Meeker notes that Wright & Kimbrough also developed the use of covenants in deeds, assuring that the neighborhood would have "desirable" set-backs from streets and bans on multi-family units, saloons, stores, and old buildings. But they also excluded African Americans and Asians, observing the "norms" regarding segregation at the time. Wright

Charles Wright and Howard Kimbrough were two of Sacramento's most prominent developers. This photograph shows one of their developments in its early stages.

& Kimbrough, and other local builders like S. Ward Ottinger, constructed custom homes in this area.

Some homes in East Sacramento, although it is not clear how many, were also built from one of the first forms of mass produced or pre-fabricated housing, the "kit" home. Mass produced housing appeared about the same time as other mass produced products. Introduced in eastern cities, the various components of the "balloon frame" house, which were constructed in Chicago, were shipped to areas of the country where local materials like timber and bricks were not readily available. Kit homes were pioneered by Otto and William Sovereign of the Aladdin Homes Company of Bay City, Michigan. The Aladdin company sold various styles of homes, especially bungalows, by retail catalogue sales. Sacramentans could order these kit homes, and once they arrived—complete with blueprint and how-to manual—the home buyer hired a local handyman to put together the structure, which could be modified. Large-scale retailers, like Montgomery Ward and Sears, Roebuck and Company, also sold these pre-fabricated homes through their catalogues.

Building South and Northeast

One of the great builders of the Curtis Park subdivision was real estate developer J. C. Carly, who was joined to the Curtis family by marriage. Beginning early in the twentieth century, Carly helped bring in improvements (including a streetcar line) to the area and then sold lots to buyers. Local builder Richard Ruiter, whose own home was in the neighborhood, erected a number of homes for homeowners. In the adjoining West Curtis Oaks subdivision, E. A. Pierce, vice president of the Oak Park Lumber Company, built a number of dwellings, favoring the bungalow style highlighted in Henry Wilson's popular *Bungalow Book*. Frank A. Williams was also a prominent Curtis Park home builder. One of his associates, Charles E. DeCuir, was another well-known and highly respected Sacramento developer.

The undeveloped areas south of downtown came to life after 1923 when the Y Street levee was removed. Y Street, later renamed Broadway, became a popular spot for development. J. C. Carly, already well-established as a land developer, noted that "Y Street at the present time is the main artery in Sacramento and probably handles more traffic than any other street in town with the possible exception of J and K." Developers followed the wake of the improvement of the area. Carly's Homeland tract, developed in 1924, consisted of a considerable number of homes, mostly bungalows and duplexes ranging in price from $4,000 to $8,000.

Wright & Kimbrough developed City Farms, rows of houses on larger lots than Oak Park. Wright & Kimbrough's 250-acre College Tract near Land Park, and the newly-erected Sacramento City College, included restrictions on size, color, decor, and racial and ethnic composition. Its marketing was targeted at Sacramentans who were looking for a low-density area to raise children: "Childhood days in College Tract will be healthy, happy days. Bright sunshine and fresh, pure air will bring rosy cheeks and sturdy bodies—while beautiful William Land Park provides a wonderful playground where kiddies may roam in perfect safety." Its advertisements related the "charm of winding boulevards, the modern improvements of artistic homes built to comply with wisely planned restrictions," promising that "you will find peace, contentment and recreation in the splendid municipal golf course of William Land Park right at your door."

J. C. Carly's Homeland development was advertised as "in direct line with the city's growth." Note also the many amenities provided for lot buyers and home builders.

Land was available to the north and east of the city. Already in the 1880s, local entrepreneurs had created Orangevale and Fair Oaks as "fruit colonies." The 1910 sale of the old Rancho del Paso, consisting of 44,000 acres, led to another wave of development. Former Sacramento Mayor Daniel Webster Carmichael established a rural colony on a portion of it. Another consortium of developers planned Citrus Heights.

North Sacramento began to develop in 1918 when the Liberty Iron Works received a government contract to produce World War I airplanes. Even though hoped-for industrial growth never materialized (the contracts were canceled when the war ended), Carl Johnston of the North Sacramento Land Company moved forward to develop the area in 1924. Thanks to steady improvements in the area's roads and interurban train system, the new suburb grew into a thriving little community. By 1926 it had water and electrical hookups, a road system of about 100 miles, four schools, and 10,000 residents. It remained a separate city until a burgeoning Sacramento annexed it in 1964.

But Del Paso Heights had been around since the days of the Great Depression, beginning as a series of shacks put up by a handful of Sacramento investors. The community's big break came in 1934 when Grant Union High School was built there, and it soon became one of the largest secondary schools in the region (and one of the first high schools in northern California to have a swimming pool). Later, when McClellan Air Force Base settled nearby, the area exploded in rows of affordable, prefabricated tract homes. In fact, Del Paso Heights grew so rapidly that in 1955 local citizens were pushing for incorporation as a sixth-class city.

The Great Depression halted the creation of new housing subdivisions. Wartime shortages further slowed the pace of growth. But this soon changed once the guns of war were silenced.

This 1928 view of the Land Park area shows the advance of development.

Postwar Developments: Suburban Expansion

Sacramento's population grew dramatically after World War II. In 1940, the county had only 170,000 residents, most of them in the city of Sacramento. By 1960, nearly 500,000 called Sacramento County home. Job opportunities made possible by the permanent presence of three large military installations (McClellan Air Force Base, Mather Air Force Base, and the Army Signal Depot) as well as private defense-related firms like Aerojet and Douglas Aircraft spurred a wave of suburban development.

The postwar real-estate boom had many fathers, but realtors Wright and Kimbrough may have kicked off the land rush when they purchased a large parcel to the northeast of the city and north of the American River named Arden Park Tract. This area, bounded by Watt Avenue, Fair Oaks Boulevard, Eastern Avenue, and Arden Way, consisted of approximately 1,900 lots in

North Sacramento began to develop when the Liberty Iron Works received a World War I contract to build airplanes. The potential prosperity promised by the new plant did not materialize, but development of the area did take place.

The credit terms advertised in this 1952 promotion of McClellan Meadows included 4 percent GI loans and generous FHA terms for non-vets.

what one retrospective press report called "a veritable land rush." The lot prices ranged from $775 to $2,000 with the average sale at about $1,200.

The successful sale of this tract was the harbinger of a fast-paced pattern of development that pushed Sacramento northeast, across the American River in the direction of the town of Folsom and the Sierra foothills. The magnet was McClellan Air Force Base, one of Sacramento's largest employers. Another shaft of development reached east along Folsom Boulevard and Highway 50 in the direction of Mather Field and Aerojet. The latter had come to Sacramento in the early 1950s and employed thousands of men and women. Subdivisions multiplied at a rate never before seen in Sacramento history. A new suburb, North Highlands, popped up very near McClellan Field. Suburban growth expanded into the Arden-Arcade area, as well as older areas such as Carmichael, Citrus Heights, Fair Oaks, and Orangevale. North Sacramento and Del Paso Heights were also caught up in this great leap forward.

The Arden Area in 1956. This part of Sacramento County filled rapidly with new homes and businesses. Note the housing developments in the right quadrant of the photo.

To the south of the city, along the west side of Highway 99, the spine of the Central Valley, working-class subdivisions called Hollywood Park, Sutterville Heights, and Freeport Village sprang up. Farther south, the small agricultural burg of Florin was quickly transformed. The eviction of Japanese farmers during World War II "freed" scores of acres for other types of development. The construction of the U.S. Army Signal Depot and the opening of the Campbell Soup plant on Franklin Boulevard reworked the dynamics of this area in the same way that McClellan and Mather Air Force Bases reworked the lands to the north. Along Florin Road, housing tracts, service stations, and supermarkets began to pop up like dandelions. By 1959, 4,000 people lived there, and speculation for even more growth ran high.

New Housing for the People

To house all these newcomers, a new cadre of real-estate dealers and builders stepped forward to meet the demand. Unlike their predecessors, postwar land developers tended to buy on a much larger scale. Here they were able to build relatively inexpensive mass produced housing, often called "tract homes," allowing many Sacramentans to realize the dream of independent home ownership.

A number of technological changes laid the groundwork for the monumental home building frenzy in Sacramento after World War II. Air conditioning, which had been installed in the state capitol in the 1930s, now became more generally available to consumers. Although it would take time for air conditioners to become a standard amenity in a new home, Sacramentans installed large swamp coolers that brought relief from the torrid summers. The increase in new houses with air conditioning required substantial expansion of the power generation capacities in the area. Federally financed water projects reworked the dynamics of the Sacramento and American Rivers. The construction of a long-awaited new dam at Folsom and a spill-off facility downriver at Nimbus assured not only water control,

These are the Capehart Homes built near McClellan Field for those stationed at the base. Military housing projects were also built at Mather Field.

but also an increase in the hydroelectric current necessary for business and residential growth.

Easy credit and government incentives to home ownership also played a major role. Low-interest Federal Housing Authority–backed loans had become available during the Great Depression and were extended after the war. The Veteran's Administration created a mortgage guarantee program in 1944, assuring mortgages without any down payment. Congress extended tax benefits to owner-occupied units. Sacramento became one of the fastest growing suburban markets in California after World War II. Many of those settling in Sacramento were returning veterans who had spent time at one of the area's military installations near the city during the war and had liked what they had seen.

By 1944, local builders had formed a trade group, the Building Industry Association of Superior California, to share information and better coordinate procurement of building materials. This organization eventually took in real-estate representatives and became a vital force in helping Sacramento builders meet the huge demand for homes after World War II.

In 1958, a total of 8,053 single-family dwelling permits were obtained for Sacramento County and the cities of Sacramento and North Sacramento. Sacramentans also built schools, created utility districts, paved roads, erected recreational facilities, and clustered around newly-formed shopping centers that became the new plazas for their communities. Sacramento's suburbs were not uniform in their housing stock, schools, or socio-economic identity. Working together with an evolving automobile culture and a network of recently-constructed federal, state, and local roads, and rows of new tract homes crowned with swamp coolers and television aerials created a virtual new city.

Mass Produced Housing

Mass produced homes, made possible by innovations in building techniques, soon began to dot Sacramento's landscape. Builder William J. Levitt pioneered a new stage of inexpensive prefabricated housing after World War II. Adapting production-line techniques to housing manufacturing,

Levitt broke down the construction of a home into 26 separate steps. For his famous Levittown on Long Island, New York, he hired teams of construction workers to level land, pave streets, and pour concrete foundation slabs. Others came to plant trees, install plumbing, and hook up electrical circuits. At each house site, trucks delivered prefabricated siding, plumbing fixtures, and wall and floor materials. Painters used spray guns to speed application, and carpenters used power instead of hand saws. Trusses, interior partitions, and door and window assemblies were also factory produced and cut to standardized shapes for quick installation on site. Teams of workers could sometimes assemble these homes in a matter of hours. The four-room wonders were only 25 by 32 feet, but they sold at an affordable $6,999.

Local builders dominated the early phase of Sacramento's mass produced housing. A number of Sacramento's developers emulated Levitt's techniques.

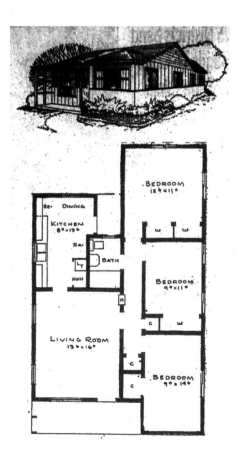

This is a floor plan that appeared in the Sacramento Bee in 1952. The newspaper ran these samples weekly to encourage suburban home buyers.

Two of the most noteworthy were Jere Strizek and Manuel Jacinto. These two and others also created residential shopping districts in the rapidly developing areas in postwar Sacramento County.

Jere Strizek and the Build-Up of the North Area

Jere Strizek was born in San Francisco in 1903 to Bohemian immigrants. After a short stint in Alaska, the elder Strizek took the family back to the old country, and young Jere was educated in Prague and Vienna. When he was high school age, the family moved back to America and settled in Seattle. Jere attended the University of Washington, majoring in civil engineering. In Seattle and Los Angeles, he started his own contracting and construction business. Strizek did well until the Depression, when his fortunes collapsed and he returned to San Francisco as a day laborer. In the spring of 1934, Strizek moved to Tracy and began building a number of homes and businesses, doing considerable work remodeling storefronts. His work won the attention of officials at the Federal Housing Authority and intrigued Sacramento auto dealer Claude Coffing who visited the builder in Tracy. Coffing, who was anxious to develop land holdings north of Sacramento, invited the builder to come to Sacramento in 1940. Strizek built his first houses at Howe Avenue and El Camino in a tract called Bohemian Village. He followed that up with more houses in the Vienna Woods development at Fulton Avenue and Bell Street.

The availability of land attracted real-estate investors like Strizek, who played a major role in the expansion of housing in the north area. In 1946, at the corner of Fulton and Marconi, Strizek opened Town & Country Village, the first major shopping center in the Sacramento area. He paid $280 per acre for its 11 original acres. The shopping center's folksy, western motif used the beams from a dismantled railroad trestle, kerosene lamps, and wagon wheels. The center included a number of popular stores and eventually grew to 22 acres. Town & Country was a catalyst to home building, and Strizek constructed nearly 1,000 homes near the site. Strizek also built homes and apartment dwellings in other parts of Sacramento County, but his greatest achievement was to build up the living areas around McClellan Air Force Base.

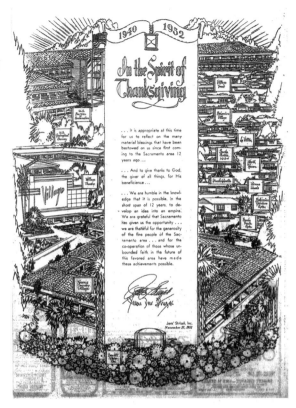

This 1952 Thanksgiving drawing provides an artistic rendition of Jere Strizek's major building projects around Sacramento.

As the vacant lands around Town & Country disappeared under the developer's hand, Strizek turned east and in 1950 purchased a 2,000-acre tract near McClellan. With the encouragement of the base commanders, he launched a series of housing projects even larger in scale than his earlier ones, building 351 homes. The developer also gave the new suburb of North Highlands its name, by combining the first words of two developments—North Haven and Highland Terrace.

Strizek eventually sold off portions of the area around McClellan to other developers. Phil Heraty and William Gannon constructed 629 homes in McClellan Meadows and 154 homes in Highland Terrace. The housing development company of Artz, Ellis & Carson constructed apartments and four-family housing units. North Highlands skyrocketed from about 150 people in 1951 to more than 22,000 eight years later. Growth was dynamic: service stations, bars, 12 churches, and 25 civic and fraternal associations took root in the new suburb along with sewer and water districts and a volunteer fire department. Nine schools "one for each year of the community's life" were in place by June of 1959. Retail outlets eagerly vied for the trade of North Highlands. At the end of the 1950s, North Highlands was a thicket of ways, drives, and boulevards (supplanting the traditional numerical streets and alphabetic avenues that were not quite as attractive). "The landscaping is coming along nicely," one *Sacramento Union* reporter noted, "but television aerials still outrank trees."

Manuel Jacinto and his Basalite Homes

Manuel Freitas Jacinto was a native of the Azore Islands. Born February 28, 1900, he came to the United States at the age of 15, settling in Sacramento. He worked with a cousin, Manuel J. Machado, a local rancher, and in 1921

This North Haven promotion included a sketch of a typical Strizek home.

110

secured employment as a carpenter. He followed that with a year or so as a brick layer and then began building homes of concrete and brick. In 1939, Jacinto bought a section of 120 lots across from McClellan Field and built 10 houses there. After these sold rapidly, he built 102 houses in the same area. During the war, he and a partner raised 100 homes in Roseville, and in 1941 he purchased 125 lots on Sacramento's Fifth Avenue and constructed 89 homes. Jacinto built Tallac Village on Fourteenth Avenue on 250 acres, which he subdivided for 850 homes. He also developed a retail center called Tallac Village Shopping Center in 1943–1944. At Fruitridge Vista he constructed 150 homes, plus another 30 homes in North Sacramento, and 105 homes in Yuba City. In Folsom on 1,700 acres, Jacinto built 22 homes and sold the remaining acres. In 1950–1951, he was selected by the U.S. government to build housing for Air Force families, the Wherry Homes near Mather Field. In 89 days, he completed 750 homes.

Jacinto utilized concrete and basalite blocks as his chief building materials. He had two floor plans and 20 elevations for each floor plan. Like Levitt, Jacinto streamlined his operation for maximum efficiency, timing the construction carefully. A typical Jacinto home had 1,882 basalite blocks that could be laid in 48 hours. Carpenters followed the masons. Including the lot, a typical home sold for less than $9,000. Until his death in 1968, Jacinto spent his leisure hours on fast motor boats or at his horse farm near Dixon.

Sacramento's Ranch-Style Homes

Scores of other builders adapted the same techniques used by Strizek and Jacinto. These were seen extensively in one of Sacramento's (and the American West's) most beloved home styles: the ranch house. This one-story residence often had an L or U shape, an open floor plan, and an attached garage. It was placed on a large enough lot to have an enclosed backyard and patio, which were accessible through a sliding glass door in the rear. The ranch style popped up everywhere, including the River Park and Arden Park tract home neighborhoods. Historian Stephen Romano notes of the postwar Tahoe Park neighborhood: "The area's ranch style, affordable, single family

Manuel Jacinto's basilite blocks created homes for thousands of Sacramentans.

two bedroom homes with large yards [were] typical for the neighborhood." Jay Parker's short-lived developments in Orangevale were also ranch style, but with more square footage and amenities than other homes. Built along the bluff of the newly-created Lake Natoma—the reservoir of the Nimbus overflow dam—they sat on capacious lots with large bedrooms, intercom systems, and two-car garages. Streets had no sidewalks, providing more space for automobile traffic.

One of Sacramento's greatest ranch-style builders was Los Angeles–based Milton J. Brock & Sons. The company was formed in 1938–1939 by Milton J. Brock, a former streetcar conductor. When Brock was fired from his job during a strike, he began the small homebuilding business with his sons Milton, Wendell, and Carroll. The firm flourished, and in 1952 they bought 400 acres in North Highlands for $400 an acre from Jere Strizek. Here they began the first Larchmont Village, one of many subdivisions of this name in the Sacramento area. In those days, Carroll Brock, the head of the Sacramento operations, recalled it took just about a year from the purchase of a subdivision to the beginning of construction. (Today it can take as long as four years.) Larchmont Homes—modest, affordable, "conventional California ranch" homes—began to sprout like mushrooms. Like most contractors, Brock sub-contracted out certain portions of the work, but they did the framing and carpentry work. Typical prices for a three-bedroom home were less than $10,000, which could be purchased without any down payment. Amenities in these new homes were few—they did not include a stove or oven, nor air conditioning, carpeting, or garbage disposal—all standard items in the company's later homes. As time went on, the size and elegance of the typical Larchmont home improved. Before selling the company in the 1990s, Larchmont Homes constructed nearly 14,000 dwellings in the Sacramento area.

Another popular designer of Sacramento homes was Mary Barden, who began designing homes for her husband John Barden, the owner of a busy construction firm. Although never formally trained as an architect, she taught herself the rudiments and designed more than 1,000 homes, including some in Sierra Oaks, Sierra Oaks Vista, South Land Park, and the College Tract. She also designed church buildings and schools and even a Carmelite Monastery on Stockton Boulevard.

One of the joys of a new Larchmont Ranch Style home was more space and privacy for the growing suburban family. The "Larchmont Larry" logo was familiar to many Sacramentans.

Larchmont Homes evolved from very simple floor plans with few amenities to larger and more appointed structures demanded by suburban home-buyers,

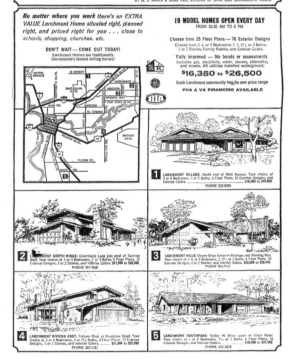

114

The 1960s and Beyond

Early developers and home builders in the first wave of Sacramento's postwar boom built with speed, but offered few floor plans or amenities. As the industry grew more sophisticated and as building materials became more readily available, mass produced housing became more varied in style, size, and comfort level. Consumers expected ranges, carpeting, and air conditioning as part of the home purchase package. Developers were willing and able to accommodate.

An early departure from the typical mass produced home in Sacramento's suburbs was showcased in South Land Park by Joseph Eichler. A wholesale dairy dealer, Eichler wanted to replicate a Frank Lloyd Wright "Usonian" house with the use of roof beams and an easy line between indoor and outdoor spaces. Working with hired architects, he began to design these homes in the San Francisco Bay Area, and in 1954 began building in South Land Park.

Eichler's work was admired by James and William Streng. Natives of Scranton, Pennsylvania, the Streng brothers had lost their father at an early age. Young Jim Streng was invited to come to California during the summers to help his uncle, Phil Heraty, a local developer who built homes in Oakland, Concord, Walnut Creek, Redding, and Chico. As noted, Heraty was a partner of William Gannon and had participated in the construction of subdivisions in North Highlands. Streng liked California, and he and his brother, an accountant, decided to go into the home building business. Their first subdivision, on Winding Way near Auburn Boulevard, was Evergreen Estates, a small cluster of ranch-style homes with conventional "crawl space" foundations, shake roofs, and a mixture of stucco and wood exteriors. The homes did not sell well at first, but eventually a group of McClellan Field officers bought them and saved the fledgling Streng operation from bankruptcy.

The brothers then bought a portion of Barrett Hills in Carmichael, where they built a model ranch-style house and also a more modernistic model, produced for them by UC Berkeley–trained architect Carter Sparks. The Strengs had investigated the appeal of the Eichler-style homes in the Bay Area

James Streng, his brother William, and architect Carter Sparks built an array of "modern" style homes in the Sacramento area.

and came back realizing they could not exactly replicate the style in this area. In 1958, they met Carter Sparks at an expectant parents' class. Sparks was himself intrigued by Eichler's designs and interested in contemporary home design. His design for the Barrett Hills home received positive responses from a group of Pacific Bell employees from the Bay Area. Over the next 30 years the Strengs worked with Sparks to produce these modernistic homes, which found a niche in the Sacramento market. Favored by lawyers, educators, tall people (they had high ceilings), and architects, these distinctive homes are known for their simple lines, use of natural light through skylights, and their tree-lined neighborhoods. The Strengs built close to 4,000 homes, mostly in the modern style, in more than 40 subdivisions and on individual lots in Sacramento and Davis. Sacramento's Wilhaggin Estates, built on 40 acres of the old Haggin Grant, contains a subdivision of these distinctive homes begun in 1967. Sheffield Oaks in Carmichael, with views of the American River, had 67 of them.

Another builder, Robert C. Powell, arrived in Sacramento in 1955 and became an admirer of Jere Strizek's Bohemian Gardens, an apartment complex just east of Town & Country Village. Impressed by Strizek's vision, Powell built his own apartment complex in 1962, the Marconi Town Houses, the first of a series of apartment complexes and townhouses. The most significant was Campus Commons, erected between 1971 and 1978. He also built the elegant Pavilions Shopping Center and was the driving force behind the upscale Gold River development near Ranch Cordova in the 1990s.

Greenhaven, in the Pocket Area to the south, developed as a residential area through the efforts of Harold Parker of the Lincoln Parker firm. This East Bay development firm was founded in 1956. Parker targeted the area in the early 1960s as the site of a planned community. Giving their development the futuristic name of "Greenhaven 70," Parker created a unique environment around a man-made lake that included greenbelt areas, a community swimming pool, parks, and other amenities to create a village-like atmosphere. Carved up by curving streets with exotic names, it was first built up with ranch-style homes. Although some of its plans did not materialize, such as a marina, it soon became a popular dwelling place for Sacramento professionals. Beginning in the 1990s the firm built Riverlake, a gated community in the Pocket Area. They also developed the Parkway in Folsom. Lincoln Parker later became the Parker Development Company, which today continues to work with planned communities like the 3,500-acre gated Serrano community in El Dorado Hills. This elegant development takes advantage of the beautiful rolling terrain of the area and provides hiking trails, a golf course, and other quality of life features that attract well-to-do residents from the San Francisco Bay Area.

An array of locally-based Sacramento home building firms dominated the market until the 1980s. These included Elliott Homes, Dunmore Development, John Mourier, J.T.S. Communities, and Winncrest Homes. Eventually, however, the production of homes in Sacramento moved toward larger, nationally-based companies.

PARK PLACE SOUTH
...By Lee Basford
Builder, Developer

In the Greenhaven/Pocket area . . . a new concept in home ownership . . .
Unruffled privacy, plus house and yard maintenance . . . at an affordable price!

━━━━━ FEATURES ━━━━━

- 2 bdrm, 2 bath
- 2 Car Garage w/Automatic Door opener
- Thermo-pane windows
- Tile Entries
- All Electric Kitchen: dishwasher microwave, self-cleaning oven, tile counters
- Instant 180° Water
- Birch Cabinetry

- Plush Carpentry
- Fireplace w/Glass Screens
- Decorator Lighting Wallpaper & Plumbing Fixtures
- Ceramic Tile Baths
- Mirror-door Wardrobes
- Front Yard Landscaping w/sprinklers
- Fenced Backyards

From $86,950

Julie Chapman
Sales Manager

Main Office 428-7853
Weekends 392-1030
Model Homes Open
Fri., Sat., Sun. & Mon. 12 to 5 p.m.

Another community from
Lee Basford, builder of fine
homes in Sacramento since 1959
*Because we are constantly improving our product, the product
design and all specifications are subject to change without notice.*

JUST 7 MIN.
FROM DOWNTOWN

The Greenhaven/Pocket area attracted several developers. Note the number of amenities that came with Lee Basford's Park Place South homes.

The Transformation of Sacramento Home Building

Several major changes transformed Sacramento's home market. The first was spatial movement. Most early postwar expansion was within Sacramento County limits, extending east toward the air bases and waking up the sleepy rural communities. Freeway and state highway expansion altered the realities of land value and access, and many housing developments began to be located near convenient off-ramps attached to Interstates 80 and 5 and also state Highways 50 and 99. Communities like Parkway Estates advertised their proximity to downtown via the freeway, while Florin Road became one of the major commercial arteries of an expanding south area.

Beginning around 1980, home building began to encompass a wider metropolitan area. To the east, Antelope and the areas around Roseville, Granite Bay, and Rocklin blossomed with new homes of various types. Winncrest Homes, a locally-based company, became one of the biggest single-family home sellers in the area in 1985. Winncrest projects were found in northeast Sacramento, El Dorado Hills, and Folsom. El Dorado County saw a spike in home building, mostly custom made homes that were easily adapted to the hilly landscape of the area. To the south, development plunged forward in the Laguna Creek area around Elk Grove where Reynen & Bardis Communities have large land holdings. North Natomas exploded in growth in the mid-1990s and continues to expand.

Steady improvements in mass produced homes, making them increasingly more elegant, have also transformed the housing market. Consumers of mass produced housing today have an amazing array of options to pick from in designing their homes. Unlike the relatively Spartan early homes of the first developers, home builders now include a level of amenities such as stone flooring, granite countertops, stainless steel appliances, engineered roofing materials, energy efficiency, and environmentally friendly construction materials. Elliott Homes, a major home builder in the Sacramento area, describes how their package includes additional bathrooms, three-car garages, tile roofs, and upgraded carpets, dishwashers, and air conditioning. Buyers of mass-produced homes in the 2000s have choices that would seem like the wildest of luxuries to those who bought early Strizek, Jacinto, or Larchmont homes in the 1950s.

Perhaps the most significant transformation of the Sacramento area housing industry has been the increasing presence of many nationally-based companies. These publicly-traded firms have become an important presence in meeting Sacramento's continuing demand for housing and accommodating its diverse income groups. Firms like Lennar, Beazer Homes, Centex, D.R. Horton, and Ryland are now well established in the Sacramento area, building homes and some commercial structures. These nationally-based organizations can take advantage of mass purchasing programs and economies of scale to deliver homes to Sacramentans that fit the budgets of most residents in the community.

Intricate interaction between land development and home building has also nuanced the Sacramento market. Some firms, such as Parker Development, deal in land sales, but also build some custom homes (Serrano). Reynen & Bardis, an important force in the development of Laguna, is primarily a development company, but also builds homes. Elliott Homes develops land and builds residential and commercial properties. Angelo Tsakopoulos, perhaps the best known land developer in the Central Valley, only buys and sells land but does not build.

As with all other branded mass produced entities, whether they are groceries, cars, or furniture, each of the home builders of Sacramento seeks to emphasize its niche in a tightly competitive market. Some emphasize their local roots and their personal investment in Sacramento. Others focus on their reputation for customer service and their attentiveness to consumer demand in housing details like energy efficiency. Still others stress their level of community investment by attention to charitable activities. Some firms, like Beazer, build smaller and simpler homes targeted at the first-time home buyer.

With all these changes, Sacramentans do, for the most part, live like kings and queens. Home ownership in Sacramento County in 2006 stood at 306,047, or 61.2 percent. Homes matter to the residents of East Sacramento, Curtis Park, and Land Park, as the quaint and distinct styles of those old neighborhoods continue to attract buyers. Some still live in the Strizek and Jacinto homes. Still others are in the larger Winncrest or Elliott Homes, or perhaps in a custom "McMansion" in Granite Bay or Los Lagos. Wherever it is, Sacramentans enjoy their homes and the benefits of home ownership.

5. "The Advantageous Display of Goods"
Department Stores and Shopping Malls

Department stores and their successors, shopping centers and malls, are concentrated images of Sacramento's culture of mass consumption. Hundreds of thousands of items from clothing to household appliances, furniture, jewelry, luggage, and bedding are on display in them. The regular changes in their advertisements and window displays signal the coming and going of holidays and mark the passing of seasons. Elegantly illustrated full-page ads and memorable radio and television commercials lure people to these stores.

Sacramento's department stores and malls are not only retail outlets, they are also social centers where people can meet, eat, and learn. A mall or shopping center spreads over a large number of acres, creating an informal crossroads for the often scattered residents. Sales statistics from these huge enterprises are one of the most important indicators of the economic health of a community. The location of a department store or mall defines the social geography of an area. The demise of a mall or replacement of its stores with different kinds of stores is also indicative of an area's socio-economic transition.

The Origins of the Department Store

Department stores began as dry goods retail operations, selling non-food items and durables like clothes, wash tubs, brooms, brushes, and other items. One of the first of these stores to appear in Sacramento, and which would evolve into a department store, was the Mechanics' Store. Opened by Polish immigrant David Lubin in October 1874, the Mechanics' Store was located above a saloon on Fourth and K Streets. Lubin's half-brother Harris Weinstock, who had some experience in retailing in San Francisco, joined him in the business. Momentous changes for the two men lay ahead.

Harris Weinstock (1854–1922), together with his half-brother David Lubin, founded one of the most successful department store operations in Sacramento. His name persisted on the company stores even after they were bought out by larger firms.

The modern department store has multiple beginnings. Some point to European origins, especially France, whose Bon Marché seemed to pioneer the basic arrangement of large emporia with various departments. Department stores were created primarily by the mass production economy, which manufactured ready-to-wear clothing and household items. The evolution of transportation systems assured a steady flow of these goods to local markets. Eventually, the idea of placing a variety of these goods under one roof, distributing them with refined merchandising processes, and promoting them with advertising developed. Other firms advanced through catalogue sales, aided by expanded mail service. Montgomery Ward, which opened in 1872, and Sears, Roebuck and Co., which began operations in 1893, were leaders in this kind of retailing. David Lubin and Harris Weinstock developed a mail-order business as well.

Some date the origin of the American department store to the founding of John Wanamaker's Philadelphia Emporium in 1876. Others point to precursors that carried a variety of manufactured goods at reasonable prices. Macy's in New York and Marshall Field in Chicago became known as major retailers. These, and other lesser known regional companies, evolved into modern department stores that eventually opened branches throughout the country. The value national chains provided to consumers was touted in a 1926 ad run in Sacramento by the National Dollar store, which introduced itself as "a great chain-department store system that lowers prices on staple commodities through a great multiple-store buying system."

Price was everything, and department store retailers did all they could to keep their products affordable and consistent. Lubin's Mechanics' Store adopted a

Labor saving home appliances were among the most popular purchases in department stores. Breuner's ad for Hotpoint vacuum cleaners also carries credit terms.

"one price" policy, a retailing innovation that had been tried in the East by Field and Wanamaker. The one-price formula, or fixed price, replaced the haggling and bargaining that had been common in dry goods retailing. As with other mass consumption industries, the availability of easy credit—installment buying and later credit cards—kept business percolating and even expanding.

In 1888 the Mechanics' Store became Weinstock, Lubin & Company and for several generations, this name was one of the most familiar to Sacramentans. Weinstock, Lubin grew larger and larger, placing its increasing stock of merchandise into separate areas, thereby becoming a modern department store. The Fourth and K site continuously increased floor space and display sophistication. In 1891, a new store was erected on the site. When this was destroyed in a 1903 fire, another opened in the same location the following year. Lubin eventually withdrew from the business to found the International Institute of Agriculture in Rome. Harris Weinstock moved away from the day-to-day oversight of the operations in 1908 when he became the state labor commissioner. After Weinstock died in 1922, Lubin's son Simon took over its management.

The Weinstock, Lubin Store at Fourth and K in 1891.

Growing demands for merchandise and the movement of the business district eastward meant another transformation for Weinstock, Lubin & Co. A 1923 land deal, brokered by downtown real-estate agent John Clecak, brought the prime property at Twelfth and K (formerly the Christian Brothers School) into the hands of Weinstock, Lubin. Soon a three-story, beaux arts, terra-cotta faced structure rose on the site, modeled on Le Printemps emporium in Paris. This new $850,000 store opened in 1924 on a 240 by 160 foot lot. "Its long street frontage . . . assures ample opportunity for show windows for the advantageous display of goods." The new Weinstock's was state-of-the-art in department stores, with each floor organized into departments and accessed by elevators and later an escalator. In addition to retailing, the store had drinking fountains, restrooms, a barber shop, a children's playroom, a hair-dressing parlor, and a beauty shop. Most importantly, "the new location of the store [placed] the firm in the center of the new shopping district and convenient to many of the new structures being erected."

Hale Brothers & Company, a San Jose firm, opened its doors in Sacramento in 1880 at Ninth and K Streets. Its location was considered chancy at the time, because it was "so far out." However, through skillful marketing, it managed to draw enough business and even anticipated the move of the central business district eastward. In 1923, it had outgrown its existing space and entered into a long-term lease with the owners of the old Clunie Hotel and Theater buildings, giving Hale's the entire half block between Eighth and Ninth along K Street. This move, plus access to the leases of the other buildings later, nearly doubled the store's size.

Charles Nathan, a native of Germany, opened a small dry goods store in 1869. Eventually, this became a successful emporium on the corner of Sixth and J Streets. Between 1904 and 1909, Nathan expanded the size and scope of the business, erecting a three-story structure with a frontage of 100 by 160 feet. Nathan was a man of many interests including extensive land holdings in Yolo County. He himself did not spend much time in Sacramento, living instead in San Francisco until the great earthquake of 1906. After that he moved to New York and later to Paris, where he purchased imported goods for his Sacramento store. He moved back to Sacramento in 1911 after the

Hale's Department Store, c. 1964.

death of his first wife, remarried in 1920, and died in 1924 at the age of 76. Nathan's building burned in 1920, and although plans were announced for a new structure farther up J Street, he decided instead to house his store in three stories of an existing six-story building at Eighth and L.

Catering to Special Needs

Department stores had a number of different, separated areas for the various items they sold. But there were also specialty stores that bought certain items wholesale for retail sale. Clothing was a favorite specialty item. For discriminating women buyers, higher-end fashions could be found at a store owned by national chain Bon Marché, which arrived in Sacramento in 1913. The San Francisco–based Ransohoff's eventually took it over. Another women's apparel store, The Nonpareil, opened in 1859 and lasted well into the twentieth century at its 610–618 K Street location. Men's apparel could be purchased at Elkus Brothers, a locally-owned clothier on K at Ninth Street.

Furniture was another specialty item that used large facilities for retail sales. John Breuner, a native of Waldangelloch, Germany, and a trained cabinet maker, came to California in 1853 in hopes of striking it rich. He, like many others, discovered it was more profitable to mine the miners. Although he had constructed sluice boxes for his fellow miners in the gold fields, he gave up his dreams of gold, returned to Sacramento, and began selling imported furniture. Breuner also sold pieces that he made himself. He announced himself to the city in August 1863 with an advertisement that read, "The people of Sacramento and of the State are informed that I intend to sell off my very large imported stock of furniture at unusually low rates as I intend to make way for goods of home manufacture. Sacramento can manufacture her own furniture and I intend to prove it."

In Sacramento, the Breuner name became synonymous with fine furnishings and quality service. Ultimately, like most retailers, Breuner sold

Hale Brothers helped to celebrate the opening of the Tower Bridge in 1935.

Breuner's delivery trucks brought purchases to Sacramento homes.

manufactured furniture. However, he continued to import furniture as well. The firm's corporate headquarters moved to Oakland in the 1930s.

National Outlets

In addition to regional or locally-based companies, Sacramento also welcomed nationwide chain stores. F. W. Woolworth opened an outlet in Sacramento in 1906 at Fifth and K Streets. A second and even larger two story Woolworth's opened at Tenth and K in 1926 and remained on the site until October 1997. Other major chains included Sears, Roebuck and Co., Montgomery Wards, and Kresge. Rosenthal's, on Fourth and K Streets, was a source for a variety of products from children's clothes to food. Sacramentans had their choice of clothing stores, in addition to the big department stores. A branch of the Federal Outfitting Company opened in Sacramento at Seventh and K Streets in 1925. This firm eventually erected a $100,000 building between Eleventh and Twelfth on J Street to accommodate its customers. The Capital

Clothing store was located directly across from the federal post office. Sears opened its first store in Sacramento in the late 1920s, directly across from Weinstock's at Twelfth and K Streets.

The Social Functions of the Department Stores

The presence of these businesses downtown assured that the center of the city remained alive and economically viable. In addition to retail shopping, department stores offered a safe locale for women who still suffered social strictures on where they could go and where they could be seen and still remain respectable. In addition to shopping, department stores also offered cooking demonstrations and beauty tips for modern women. In 1926, the Hale Brothers store welcomed Mme. Ida Chernoff, "a nationally known authority," who presented a series of lectures on

This is Breuner's store on Sixth and K after 1929 remodeling.

"Health, Beauty and Psychology." In a lecture in the store's fourth floor auditorium aimed at "every woman, whether parent, housewife, business woman, society matron, or aspirant for political work," she promised to help them "get what [they] want. Whether it is the love of your friends, or money or business achievement, you can have your most heartfelt desires granted." Chernoff's free lectures provided tips on hair care, the use of perfume, and even proper posture. Weinstock's offered "A Short Course in Short Cuts in Home Sewing," directed by Emily Harley, who was in charge of the cutting and fitting service. Harley was assisted by Martha Jane Gray of the Educational Department of the Singer Sewing Machine Company.

Department stores also provided a window on the wider world for Sacramentans who began to vacation more regularly in the 1920s. A "Travel Show" sales campaign spotlighted a week of travelogue movies, slides, and lectures, highlighting scenic Western sites such as Glacier and Yosemite

Woolworth's on K Street was a popular shopping venue for many years.

This seasonal display was in Weinstock's.

Parks, railroad trips to the Rockies, and steamship cruises to Europe and Japan. Department store windows became urban showplaces, and seasonal displays at Breuner's and Weinstock's became an important part of holiday traditions. The Retail Merchant's Association coordinated an annual fall roll-out of new products, which was accompanied by a competition for the best window display. This autumn event brought hundreds of window shoppers downtown.

Going to the department store was often an outing for a Sacramento family. Men and women often dressed for the occasion in suits, jackets, hats, and gloves. One Sacramentan, Jim Keating, remembered visiting Weinstock's in 1940: "I had a lot of fun at Weinstock Lubin," recalled Keating. "Back in the forties they had the first escalator in Sacramento and it was a new thing to ride up and down when we were kids."

This 1908 photograph shows customers and clerks in the Weinstock store.

A New Commercial Geography: Shopping Centers and Early Malls

Even as downtown flourished, Sacramento's steady growth outward, first to the east and then to the northeast, gradually shifted its shopping districts away from the urban center. Already in the 1920s, noted a *Bee* reporter, city road building had begun to open "many of the hitherto dormant sections of Sacramento." City manager H. C. Bottdorf observed of the homes springing up along a newly-paved H Street from Forty-Seventh Street to the east levee at Fifty-Seventh Street: "This means a tremendous increase in the business value of the city, as in each new territory opened a trade district has established itself."

The significant and fast-paced changes of the post–World War II period provided a new context for every aspect of Sacramento life. Sacramento was no longer a small community bound by a handful of common institutions and personal ties. Indeed, its sheer growth and diversity seemed to fracture the city into a thousand different pieces. Old patterns of association born of common schooling, church, or commercial associations became obsolete. The new Sacramento was larger, more spatially diffuse, transient (thanks to the coming and going of military and defense workers), and wealthy. To some degree, the shopping center and the mall reflected these new social realities. These commercial centers, rather than the downtown, became the new public plazas—gathering spots for community events, the place to see and be seen, and a cheap form of recreation for Sacramento families who had enough disposable income to spend on consumer goods. A later decision to locate movie theaters near suburban malls added to their attraction.

The Decline of the Downtown Shopping District

The downtown shopping districts that had been the pride and joy of the urban planners of the 1920s suffered a steady decline in patronage. One by one, the many stores along the J and K Street retail district went out of business. Some of these stores, like Weinstock's and Breuner's, followed the flood of migration out to the suburbs and kept their names alive in

These ads from the Arden Town grand opening capitalized on its proximity to the Country Club District and Carmichael.

shopping centers and various other locations for a time, until even they went under.

Weinstock's remained a family business until rival Hale Brothers bought a controlling interest in the company in 1930. It retained the Weinstock name. In 1951, Hale Brothers merged with the Broadway Department Stores of Los Angeles, and in 1965 Hale's and Weinstock's merged into one Northern California Division under the Broadway-Hale Corporation structure until it was bought out by Federated Department Stores Inc., which owned Macy's and Bloomingdale's, ending 120 years of retail history. Under a reorganization plan, the Weinstock's stores, anchors for three Sacramento area malls—Arden Fair, Country Club Plaza, and Sunrise—were renovated and converted to Macy's. Others were simply closed, and the name Weinstock's passed into history.

Breuner's remained in the family until 1968 when the company went public. In 1978, the retail giant Marshall Field & Co. acquired it. It was subsequently taken over by BAT (British-American Tobacco), which has an American retailing arm, BATUS Retailing Group. Prism Capital, a New York merchant bank, bought Breuner's in 1990. In 1993, the company filed for bankruptcy protection. In 1994, Arnold's Home Furnishing, a San Diego firm, bought all nine Breuner's stores; however, the Breuner's name disappeared totally in 2005 when a bankruptcy court dissolved it once and for all.

By the time these once-great local stores went out of existence, many Sacramentans either had never heard of them or only knew them from suburban outlets. By then there were new venues for buying and selling.

The Postwar Shopping Centers

The modern shopping center, which later evolved into the enclosed mall, represents a major transformation in the evolution of marketing. These retail centers were created as a result of the increased use of the automobile in the United States. One of the first, called Country Club Plaza (the same name a Sacramento center would take years later), was developed in 1922 in Kansas City, Missouri.

Sacramento's love affair with the automobile dramatically transformed the region and created new opportunities for suburban living and shopping as smaller shopping centers began to pop up around the developing residential areas. In 1946, home builder Jere Strizek opened the rustic Town & Country Village, as noted, one of the first major shopping centers in Sacramento County. By 1949 Town & Country had 60 stores, a thriving restaurant (Chuck Wagon), and a nearby theater (the Village)—"without so much as one neon sign!" wrote one commentator. "Sacramentans are just as proud of it as Angelenos are of the Wilshire Boulevard Miracle Mile or the super Crenshaw shopping center."

The Work of James J. Cordano

One of Sacramento's greatest retail developers was James J. Cordano. A son of Italian immigrants, he was born in Sacramento in 1904, and at age 18 began his real-estate career as a rent collector for the Dan Carmichael

Town & Country Village, built by Jere Strizek in 1946, continues to be a popular shopping venue for Sacramentans.

James J. Cordano founded the Cordano Company in 1922. It became one of the area's greatest shopping center developers. (Courtesy Cordano Company.)

Company where he developed special expertise in leasing chain stores. He opened his own business in 1943 and brokered leases on K Street, which continued to thrive as Cordano signed on retailers like Woolworth, Joseph Magnin, and Kinney Shoes.

Trends in marketing and retail sales in America were in a continual state of flux after World War II. Already in 1950, Northgate Center, a regional shopping center near Seattle, had opened. Anchored by a Bon Marché department store, it included more than 800,000 square feet along a pedestrian walkway or "mall" for its other stores. Other growing metropolitan areas were providing similar retail centers for their burgeoning suburbs. Cordano caught the crest of the wave in Sacramento, providing new shopping centers for the expanding population. Working with the

San Francisco–based Blumenfeld Enterprises, he helped to create Country Club Centre in 1952 on a 13-acre site on Watt Avenue—the area's first regional shopping mall. It was anchored by two major department stores, J. C. Penney's and the Tacoma-based Rhodes Brothers. Country Club, with its huge parking lot ringed by palm trees and a series of shops, was an instant hit.

In 1960, another mall was built on 30 acres directly across Watt Avenue from Country Club Centre. A $6 million Weinstock's and an F. W. Woolworth's store anchored the new open-air Country Club Plaza. Not far from both Country Clubs was Arden Fair, destined to be one of the most popular in the Sacramento area. The Kassis brothers, well-known grocers, played a significant role in its creation. They, like other mall developers, made sure that their retail outlets were close to the communities' transportation arteries: the freeways.

This is the Weinstock's store that was an anchor for Country Club Plaza.

Arden Fair

The story of Arden Fair reflects the significance of informal ties of association that once characterized Sacramento business life. Frank Kassis recalled meeting the local Sears manager, "Fuzz" Bullock, at a Lions Club event. The two became fast friends, and on one occasion they took a car ride to the area where Arden Way met the freeway. Bullock confided to Kassis that Sears had done a survey of the Sacramento metropolitan area and decided to locate a store there. To approach a retail grocer with plans for a mall might seem unusual today, but in the 1950s malls included grocery operations. In fact, the Kassis brothers had opened a Stop 'n Shop near Country Club Centre. With their keen knowledge of local conditions and their network of business friends and associates, the Kassis brothers

Arden Fair Shopping center was one of the largest in the area for many years. The Kassis Brothers Food Circus was a popular addition to the shopping center.

enjoyed a degree of credibility and respectability within the Sacramento business community.

Developers Phil Heraty and William Gannon controlled the parcel on Arden Way. Gannon and Heraty soon contacted Kassis and urged him and his brothers to take the lead in developing a major shopping center there. The location had excellent freeway access and was close to a major motel, the Sacramento Inn. Kassis worked his contacts with department store heads and eventually William Ahern of Hale's passed the proposal on to Edward Carter, the president of the Broadway-Hale parent company. Carter agreed to add Hale's, which then joined Sears as the second anchor store. However, it took nearly two years to negotiate leases for the rest of the stores. Eventually See's Candy, Kress, Lane Bryant, and Woolworth signed leases. The Kassis brothers themselves also invested in Arden Fair Mall by opening what would today be called a food court, Food Circus. In a 1964 retrospective, Frank Kassis commented on the sheer size of Arden Fair, noting to the press that the 83.5 acre site, if superimposed on downtown Sacramento, "would extend from Sixth Street to beyond Sixteenth in a wide strip covering K Street and reaching from J to L."

Florin Center and Sunrise Mall

In 1960, Cordano again joined with Blumenfeld Enterprises to bring a mall to the developing south side of the city. Southgate Mall on Florin Road and Franklin Boulevard began in 1960 with great hopes of becoming the main retailer in the fast developing area near Parkway Estates.

However, during the mid-1950s, mall architecture was shifting. New developments were pioneered by Austrian-born designer Victor Gruen, who had designed Northland Mall near Detroit. This operation clustered two levels of buildings around a common, enclosed central space. In 1956, Gruen built the first fully-enclosed shopping center in Edina, Minnesota.

Enclosed malls became the trend. James Cordano sold out his interest in Southgate and invested in a new project one mile east of the complex called

This rendering of the Florin Center Mall shows its anchors J. C. Penney's, Weinstock's, and Sears.

Florin Center—Sacramento's first enclosed shopping mall. Sixty acres, located strategically close to the proposed south Sacramento freeway, were purchased from Parkway Estates for $700,000. Florin Center, with anchor stores Sears, Weinstock's, and J. C. Penney's, opened in 1967 with parking for 6,000 vehicles.

In the early 1970s, in one of the riskiest moves of his career, James Cordano located a new mall in the eastern part of the county away from a freeway off-ramp, hoping that the population would grow along Sunrise Boulevard (then a two-lane road) in Citrus Heights. The new Sunrise Mall attracted 103 stores, including four major anchors: J. C. Penny, Liberty House, Weinstock's, and Montgomery Wards. There were parking accommodations for 6,500 vehicles. Cordano's gamble paid off handsomely. When it opened in April 1972, Sunrise Mall was an immediate success and a thriving commercial district filled in around it. Roads were widened, restaurants and other service industries opened, and where there had once been pasture land, there was now the roar of automobiles and the whir of cash registers. In its shadow other malls developed, including the 39 acre open-air Birdcage Walk across the street, and Fountain Square down the street. Sunrise Mall's success encouraged the community of Citrus Heights to incorporate, with a portion of its revenues coming from the sales tax generated by the mall.

Proposition 13 and the Rise of the Big-Box Stores

Sunrise Mall and other retail centers, with the ability to generate vast amounts of tax income, became a boon to the community, as did other major retailers in the wake of Proposition 13—the 1978 landmark property tax reduction initiative. In the wake of the new legislation, local governments, anxious for tax revenues, encouraged mega-retailers and their huge sales volume. Like auto malls, big-box stores were important sources of revenue. Wal-Mart, the Arkansas-based giant headed by Sam Walton, moved into the Sacramento region in November 1991 when it opened a store in Elk Grove. Opposition from local merchants and strategic planning by the firm kept these stores outside Sacramento city limits for a time, but their locations soon encircled the downtown. This was followed by stores in North Highlands, Rocklin, and Folsom. Eventually, the site of the old Country Club Centre and Southgate Plaza shopping center became homes to Wal-Mart stores. Wal-Mart's membership-only branch, Sam's Club, also opened stores on Stockton Boulevard, El Camino Avenue, and Sunrise Boulevard, as well as in Rancho Cordova and Roseville. Wal-Mart would later become the anchor for a new generation of shopping centers like Natomas Marketplace. Price Costco—or simply Costco—began with a membership warehouse, Price Club, on Watt Avenue. In 1995 it acquired 22 acres adjacent to the Radisson Hotel on Leisure Lane and built a thriving warehouse store on Expo Parkway.

The Next Generation: Failure and Make Overs

Changes in markets and demographics launched a new wave of restructuring and mall renovations and innovations in the 1980s. Town & Country Village did not have anchor stores nor did it seek to enclose its shopping venues within an air conditioned shell. Town & Country kept its rustic look and tile roof (although a fire caused major damage and required repairs to the original Strizek buildings). It continued to prosper nonetheless, because nearby businesses built retail traffic and even imitated the Town & Country motif. Eventually specialty stores like William Glen, with gourmet delights like roasted coffee, designer kitchenware, and china attracted an upscale crowd. In fact, Glen was later described as an anchor store when the center embarked on a $4 million expansion in 1987. Longtime tenants included a doughnut shop, a pharmacy, and other lower price outlets. Economic hard times and problems in the area began to reduce its attractiveness, but Starbucks and Jamba Juice remained popular and attracted a drive-in crowd. Trader Joe's, a specialty grocery chain, built a large store giving the center a more eclectic mix.

Marvin L. "Buzz" Oates, a legendary Sacramento developer, came to the assistance of the ailing Country Club Centre when he purchased it in the 1980s. Both Watt Avenue–based Country Club malls had suffered from the lack of ready access to the freeway. At Country Club Centre, Wal-Mart

The newly remodeled Arden Fair Mall.

spent millions to convert the old two-story Montgomery Ward store, and Oates himself sought tenants to replace other businesses that had departed. Country Club Plaza, across the street, was enclosed in 1970–1971 and added an auto repair center and later a J. C. Penney's store as anchors. One reporter described it as "a fortress of commerce surrounded by a moat of blacktop roofing." When Penney's departed for a new location at Arden Fair in 1989, it was replaced by Fresno-based Gottschalks. The former Weinstock's store became a Macy's in the mid-1990s. Decline continued until 2001 when Scottsdale-based Arizona Partners purchased it, and in 2002 it was "re-malled" and re-opened in December 2003 with Bed, Bath and Beyond as an anchor.

Oates had done the same for Southgate Plaza, which had floundered since its rival Florin Center opened. In 1983, Oates bought the property for $9.6 million and resuscitated the ailing complex by bringing in important national discount chains such as Ross, Federated Group, Home Club, Sports Club, and Shoe Factory. Oates sold it to a group of Los Angeles investors for $30.5 million. The center managed to keep afloat once Albertson's market and Wal-Mart relocated there. By 2007 all of these stores had moved on, with the exception of Wal-Mart, which is planning a move in 2008.

Florin Center did not have such luck, and it faded under intense competition from Arden Fair and the Downtown Plaza, as well as population shifts toward Elk Grove further south. Anchor stores pulled out, leaving gaping holes in its retail space. Soon other retailers moved out as well, leaving only about half of the original 85 spaces still in operation in 2006. At that point, the San Francisco–based Sac LLC purchased the property, razed the 667,000 square foot interior mall, and made way for a Wal-Mart Supercenter and an open-air mall called Florin Towne Center.

At Sunrise Mall, time and customers had taken their toll on the 1970s-era buildings. James Cordano himself launched a $10 million face-lift project, which involved increasing the amount of natural lighting by replacing large portions of the ceilings with giant strips of skylights and huge glass domes. No additional square footage was added, but the effort was a clear indication of the desire to keep up with the continued demand for new and improved retail outlets, as well as for merchants to provide different kinds of space and lighting in marketing their wares and attracting consumers.

In 1988, an aging Arden Fair rolled out plans for a substantial renovation, adding a second shopping level and increasing its square footage from 589,700 feet to just over one million square feet. The renovated center featured 200 stores plus remodeled anchors Sears and Weinstock's (later Macy's). It also managed to attract the upscale clothier Nordstrom. Opening in phases beginning with the refurbished Sears in March 1989, followed by the 184,000 square foot Nordstrom at center stage. Its final wing debuted in mid-1990 and included a food court and a mix of stores for everything from jewelry to electronics. The rebuilt Arden Fair mall is still a very popular Sacramento shopping destination.

Bringing the Mall Downtown

Victor Gruen, who had pioneered the enclosed mall, believed that a downtown pedestrian mall could revitalize urban centers. In 1959, he designed Burdick Mall in Kalamazoo, Michigan, and according to one historian "inspired a national craze for downtown pedestrian malls." The redevelopers of downtown Sacramento had similar plans in mind for Sacramento's declining center. Already in the mid-1960s, K Street from Seventh to Thirteenth was becoming a modern walking/shopping area in the heart of the city. Sculpture fountains, which came to be labeled "tank traps," were placed along the walkway. Eventually, these were removed when the light rail system was built. The hoped-for renaissance of the downtown shopping district never materialized.

One effort to draw shoppers back downtown included creating an urban version of the shopping mall. The Downtown Plaza, linked to the expanding Interstate system, began with the opening of Macy's in 1963. A Holiday Inn and Weinstock's sought to anchor the site on redeveloped land on the west end of K Street.

In 1989, local developers of the Downtown Plaza advanced a plan conceived by Ernest W. Hahn and architect Louis Jerde to expand the shopping area at the foot of K Street by 250,000 square feet. They conceived

Macy's Department Store opened downtown in 1963.

an outdoor plaza with parking, food, and entertainment as well as specialty shops, to lure customers back to the downtown area. Downtown Plaza opened in 1993. Connected to Old Sacramento by a tunnel, the "malling" of Sacramento had finally come back to a spot very near the city's original retail district. Downtown Plaza ultimately came under the direction of the Australian-based Westfield Company.

The Next Wave: Giant Mega Malls

As Sacramento's population moved eastward, smaller shopping centers emerged near residential developments. Folsom developed Broadstone Mall along Highway 50 and Bidwell Street. More upscale shopping centers, which included elegant dining and specialty shops, were to be found in El Dorado Hills. In North Natomas, Natomas Marketplace, located off I-80 and Truxel Road, has tried to keep pace with the explosive housing market in that area. Along Jefferson Boulevard in West Sacramento, a retail center is anchored by Target and a Nugget food market.

Ultimately, mall retailing felt the trend toward giantism reflected in both food and automobile markets—the Mega Mall, spreading out over hundreds of acres and resembling a small village. Market surveys revealed that a large pocket of wealthy consumers was forming in eastern Placer County. The booming community of Rocklin, once a small rural burg, made the first bid to develop a mega mall in it environs around Granite Drive. Legal troubles and protests from environmentalists and residents of nearby Loomis stymied those plans.

Plans shifted to vacant lands near Roseville, now a growing bedroom community of Sacramento and close to one of the area's major employer's, Hewlett Packard. In August 2000, the Westfield Company opened its giant mall, the Westfield Galleria, in Roseville. Dwarfing any then in existence in the area, this 1.1 million square foot, upscale regional mall housed 120 retail and specialty stores and employed more than 2,000 people. It opened to gala celebrations. Rather than the boxy designs of Sunrise and Arden, Galleria's architecture included what James Czech, president of Urban Retail Properties, called "California Eclectic," which included Greek Revival-inspired arches. A portion of Harding Road on which the mall was located was renamed Galleria Boulevard. Upscale restaurants like Il Fornaio and home decor stores catering to the needs of the huge residences being built in and around the area were in evidence: Crate and Barrel, Pottery Barn, Restoration Hardware, and Williams Sonoma. The annual receipts and sales tax revenue for the Galleria were astounding, and traffic congestion continues to plague the nearby roadways.

Other areas of Sacramento County, such as the proposed Lent Ranch regional mall in Elk Grove (the Elk Grove Promenade), have met with some resistance from local residents who fear the added traffic, noise, and pollution a gigantic mall would bring. After being rejected by the county's planning commission in 1999, the project received new life when Elk Grove attained cityhood in July 2000. Nonetheless, the hurdles continued with protests from environmentalists, citizen groups, and competitors who fought against the project. Finally in late spring 2007, the Elk Grove Planning Commission approved plans for the Elk Grove Promenade, an open-air shopping center (national trends indicating enclosed malls being out of favor with consumers) with as much square footage as Roseville's Galleria.

Developer General Growth Properties, Inc. (the second largest U.S.-based, publicly-traded, real estate investment company) broke ground on the Elk Grove project in September 2007. Anchored by Macy's, Barnes & Noble, and a 16-screen theater, the mall's sales tax revenues are anticipated to reach $3.6 million during its first year of operation. It will also provide 2,500 jobs. Louis Bucksbaum, vice president of development for General Growth, stated that the "Elk Grove Promenade will be a shopping destination and gathering place for Northern California." Elk Grove's mayor, Jim Cooper, cited the mall as "a major amenity." Area residents welcomed the convenience of not having to drive to Arden Fair, Sunrise Mall, or Roseville's Galleria.

Although nothing is inevitable, history has shown that Sacramentans are fixed in their habits of consumption. Malls and shopping centers may be curtailed and modified, but only rarely will they be stopped.

AFTERWORD

This small book only scratches the surface of mass consumption in the Sacramento area. Even within the narrowly defined scope of transportation, food, shelter, clothing, and household appliances, there have been many other stores and businesses where Sacramentans have sold and shopped. Other venues of mass consumption such as entertainment, including live theater, movies, sports, and fairs, claim millions of Sacramento dollars each year. New retail areas in Elk Grove and the old railroad yards will add locations where local citizens can gather to shop and socialize. It is the author's hope that some scholar or enterprising graduate student will write a more substantial account of this phenomenon.

Hopefully this brief sketch opens a small window into the collective identity of Sacramentans. While not the only feature of the local culture, it is an important one. Advertisers and others study what motivates us as individuals and as a society. They not only create needs through their skillful and strategic use of promotions, but they use symbolic language and images to touch deeper desires.

Since mass consumption became a defining feature of American life in the twentieth century, there has been an almost continuous argument about its impact on our way of life. The spectrum of opinions stretch from those who decry American consumerism as a sign of cultural decadence to those who celebrate it as the fulfillment of the American dream—as evidence of the good life to which all can legitimately aspire. Whatever one's position on the deeper meaning, consumption remains a fascinating aspect of the culture of modern Americans and Sacramentans. To some extent, we are what we consume.

BIBLIOGRAPHY

This book represents original research in a broader field that has a number of distinguished scholars. I consulted these works as I prepared this text. In the absence of traditional footnotes, I would like to acknowledge the scholars whose ideas I have quoted or used.

Newspaper Articles Cited by Chapter

Introduction

"An Entertaining and Interesting Old World." *Sacramento Bee*, June 10, 1925: 30.

Chapter 1

Sterling Forest advertisement. *Sacramento Bee*, November 28, 1925: 11.

"Women Are in a Class By Themselves When it Comes to Bargain Hunts." *Sacramento Bee*, September 20, 1921: 25.

"The Man who Dares to Go on Shopping Tour with Wifey Now is Rare Bird." *Sacramento Bee*. September 16, 1920: 4.

Chapter 2

"Statistics Give Sacramento Lead Over All in Number of Automobiles per Inhabitant." *Sacramento Bee*, October 30, 1926: A1.

"New Model Fever Has Grip on Sacramento Auto Row." *Sacramento Bee*, August 28, 1940: 17.

"Registrations of Cars Again Will Top 60,000 Mark." *Sacramento Bee*, August 29, 1940: A7.

"5,735 Is Total Sacramento Car Sales in 1925." *Sacramento Bee*, February 10, 1926: 16.

"Merely Some Private Thinks." *Sacramento Bee*, July 6, 1925: 22.

"Auto is Factor in Progress of American Home." *Sacramento Bee*, April 26, 1926: 32.

"31st Street to Be Made Retail Business Area." *Sacramento Bee*, December 10, 1925: 1, 2.

"Jacobs Company to Build Branch at 30th and J." *Sacramento Bee*, March 18, 1926: 1.

"Arden Arcade Backers Want Auto Dealer Revenue to Stay in Community." *Sacramento Bee*, May 4, 2007: B1.

"Dealerships on the Move." *Sacramento Business Journal*, September 21, 2007.

Chapter 3

Piggly Wiggly advertisement. *Sacramento Bee*, April 2, 1926: 2.

"Grocery Firms Are Moving out into Residence District." *Sacramento Bee*, November 13, 1926: A2.

Chapter 4

"Residential Development Covers Bulk of City Area." *Sacramento Bee*, May 4, 1929: A1.

"Many Homes are being Purchased by Working Men." *Sacramento Bee*, September 5, 1925: A5.

"Public Looks for Comfort in Home." *Sacramento Bee*, January 2, 1926: A4.

"City is Expanding to East and South." *Sacramento Bee*, November 21, 1925: A4.

Land Park advertisement. *Sacramento Bee*, April 5, 1926: 16.

Chapter 5

National Dollar store advertisement. *Sacramento Bee*, April 5, 1926: 13.

Hale Brothers advertisement. *Sacramento Bee*, May 7, 1926: 3.

Weinstock's advertisement. *Sacramento Bee*, August 18, 1926: 6.

Travel Show advertisement. *Sacramento Bee*, May 15, 1926: 6.

"City Business Scope Widened by Opened Streets in New Tracts." *Sacramento Bee*, November 7, 1925: A4.

"Developer Breaks Ground on Elk Grove Mall." *Sacramento Business Journal,* September 20, 2007.

Other Works Consulted

Books

Cohen, Lizabeth. *A Consumers' Republic: The Politics of Mass Consumption in Postwar America.* New York: Alfred A. Knopf, 2003.

Cross, Gary. *An All-Consuming Century: Why Commercialism Won in Modern America.* New York: Columbia University Press, 2000.

Farrell, James J. *One Nation Under Goods.* Washington, D.C.: Smithsonian Books, 2003.

Glickman, Lawrence B., ed. *Consumer Society in American History: A Reader.* Ithaca, NY: Cornell University Press, 1999.

Kowinski, William S. *The Malling of America.* New York: Morrow, 1985.

Leach, William. *Land of Desire: Merchants, Power, and the Rise of a New American Culture.* New York: Pantheon Press, 1993.

Marchand, Roland. *Advertising the American Dream: Making Way for Modernity, 1920–1940.* Berkeley: University of California Press, 1985.

McGowan, Joseph A. *History of the Sacramento Valley,* vol. II. New York: Lewis Historical Publishing Company, 1961.

Schmidt, Leigh Eric. *Consumer Rites: The Buying and Selling of American Holidays.* Princeton, NJ: Princeton University Press, 1995.

Starr, Kevin. *Coast of Dreams: California on the Edge, 1990–2003.* New York: Alfred A. Knopf, 2004.

Strasser, Susan. *Satisfaction Guaranteed: The Making of the American Mass Market.* Washington, D.C.: Smithsonian Institution Press, 1989.

Veblen, Thorstein. *The Theory of the Leisure Class.* Dover Publications, 1994.

Wilson, Henry L. *The Bungalow Book: Floor Plans and Photos of 112 Houses, 1910.* Dover Publications, 2006.

Yee, Alfred. *Shopping at Giant Foods: Chinese American Supermarkets in Northern California.* Seattle, WA: University of Washington Press, 2003.

Journal Articles

Hanchett, Thomas W. "U.S. Tax Policy and the Shopping Center Boom of the 1950s and 1960s." *American Historical Review* 101 No. 4, October 1996, 1082-1110.

Nickles, Shelly. "More is Better: Mass Consumption, Gender and Class Identity in Post-War America." *American Quarterly* 54 No. 4, December 2002, 581-622.

Swiencicki, Mark A. "Consuming Brotherhood: Men's Culture, Style and Recreation as Consumer Culture, 1880–1930." *Journal of Social History* 31 No. 4, Summer 1998, 773-808.

Tomes, Nancy. "Merchants of Health: Medicine and Consumer Culture in the United States, 1900–1940." *Journal of American History* 88 No. 2, September 2001, 519-547.

Encyclopedia Articles

Kahn, H. Hezel. "Consumerism and Consumption." *Encyclopedia of Historians and Historical Writing*, vol. 1. Chicago: Fitzroy Dearborn, 1999.

Laird, Pamela Walker. "Consumerism." *Encyclopedia of American Culture and Intellectual History*, vol. 3. New York: Charles Scribner & Sons, 2001.

Strasser, Susan. "Consumption." *Encyclopedia of the United States in the Twentieth Century*, vol. 3. New York: Charles Scribner & Sons, 1996.

Assorted Publications

60th Anniversary Building Industry Association of Superior California, 1944–2004. BIA Publication.

Anthonisen, Marion. "If the Shoe Fits." *Prosper*. October 2007, 98-101.

Bowker, Michael. "Blue Diamond Comes Out of its Shell." *Prosper*. October 2007, 88-92.

Meeker, Amanda Paige. "Wright and Kimbrough Tract 24: Review of National Register Eligibility." Sacramento: Master's thesis, California State University Sacramento, 2000.

Praetzellis, Adrian Charles. "The Archaeology of a Victorian City: Sacramento,

California." Berkeley: Ph.D. dissertation, University of California, 1991.

Praetzellis, Mary; and Adrian Praetzellis. "The Mary Collins Assemblage: Mass Marketing and the Archaeology of a Sacramento Family." Cultural Resources Facility, Anthropological Studies Center, Sonoma State University.

Romano, Stephen David. "The Dynamics of Community: A Case Study of the Tahoe Park Neighborhood Association Sacramento, California." Sacramento: Master's thesis, California State University Sacramento, 1996.

"To the Stock Holders, Weinstock, Lubin & Co." February 14, 1912. Annual Reports of Harry Thorp, 83/45/12-17.

Vanishing Victorians: A Guide to Historic Homes of Sacramento. Sacramento: American Association of University Women, 1973.

INDEX